WRITTEN AND INTERPERSONAL COMMUNICATION METHODS FOR LAW ENFORCEMENT

Second Edition

WRITTEN AND INTERPERSONAL COMMUNICATION METHODS FOR LAW ENFORCEMENT

HARVEY WALLACE
Professor
California State University
Fresno, California

CLIFF ROBERSON
Professor
Washburn University
Topeka, Kansas

CRAIG STECKLER
Chief of Police
Fremont, California

Upper Saddle River, New Jersey 07458

Library of Congress Cataloging-in-Publication Data

Wallace, Harvey.
    Written and interpersonal communication methods for law enforcement / Harvey
  Wallace, Cliff Roberson, Craig Steckler.--2nd ed.
      p. cm.
    Includes bibliographical references and index.
    ISBN 0-13-028494-7
      1. Communication in police administration. 2. Communication in law enforcement. 3.
  Interpersonal communication. I. Roberson, Cliff, 1937-II. Steckler, Craig. III. Title.

HV7936.C79 W35 2001
363.2'01'4--dc21   00-034654

Publisher: *Dave Garza*
Acquisitions Editor: *Kim Davies*
Production Editor: *Lori Dalberg, Carlisle Publishers Services*
Production Liaison: *Barbara Marttine Cappuccio*
Director of Manufacturing & Production: *Bruce Johnson*
Managing Editor: *Mary Carnis*
Manufacturing Buyer: *Ed O'Dougherty*
Art Director: *Marianne Frasco*
Cover Design Coordinator: *Miguel Ortiz*
Cover Designer: *Wanda España*
Cover Art: *Heidi Merscher/SIS/Images.com*
Marketing Manager: *Chris Ruel*
Editorial Assistant: *Lisa Schwartz*
Interior Design and Composition: *Carlisle Communications, Ltd.*
Printing and Binding: *R. R. Donnelley & Sons*

Prentice-Hall International (UK) Limited, *London*
Prentice-Hall of Australia Pty. Limited, *Sydney*
Prentice-Hall Canada Inc., *Toronto*
Prentice-Hall Hispanoamericana, S.A., *Mexico*
Prentice-Hall of India Private Limited, *New Delhi*
Prentice-Hall of Japan, Inc., *Tokyo*
Prentice-Hall Singapore Pte. Ltd.
Editora Prentice-Hall do Brasil, Ltda., *Rio de Janeiro*

10 9 8 7 6 5 4 3 2 1
ISBN 0-13-028494-7

To Randa

To Lynne

To Casey

Contents

Preface

The success of the first edition has provided us with the opportunity to improve the text. As noted in the first edition, three individuals with differing backgrounds in the criminal justice system have combined their experience in writing this text. One has experience as a defense attorney, another is a former prosecutor and city attorney, and the third is a chief of police. Their varied backgrounds provide the reader with a broad-based approach to communication in the law enforcement profession.

The main purpose of this book is to improve your communication skills, both oral and written. A secondary purpose is to improve your ability to complete the reports and forms commonly used in the criminal justice system. The best way to improve communication skills is by practicing those skills correctly. Throughout this text, you will be asked to read background material, work through exercises, correct improper English, and refine your skills.

At the end of each chapter is a section entitled "Better Writing Drills." These sections review English grammar rules and give other writing improvement tips. In addition, each chapter includes a list of frequently used words to improve your spelling. In several chapters, we also include checklists regarding the various types of communication necessary for criminal justice professionals. If you follow our recommendations and the procedures contained in this text, your verbal and written communications skills should both improve.

We would like to thank the following reviewers of the first edition for their comments: Maria Haberfield, Ph.D., Jersey City State College; Carl E. Russell,

Scottsdale Community College, and Dr. Richard Martin, Elgin Community College. We would also like to express our appreciation to the following law enforcement professionals and their agencies for supplying material and/or comments which assisted in preparing this text:

LAW ENFORCEMENT AGENCIES IN THE UNITED STATES

Supervisory Special Agent Lester A. Davis
Federal Bureau of Investigation
FBI Academy
Quantico, Virginia
   and
Carla Liverman
Technical Information Specialist
Federal Bureau of Investigation
FBI Academy
Quantico, Virginia

Quartermaster Calvin J. Avery
Harbor Police Department
Port of New Orleans
New Orleans, Louisiana

Colonel R. G. Engels
Chief of Police
Division of Police
County of Henrico, Virginia
   and
Officer P. T. MacRae
Planning Unit
Division of Police
County of Henrico, Virginia

Donald C. Taylor
Chief of Police
Fort Smith Police Department
Fort Smith, Arkansas

and
Captain David Chapman
Administrative Assistant
Fort Smith Police Department
Fort Smith, Arkansas

Richard V. Ottman
Chief of Police
Huntsville, Alabama

Director James R. Wilson
Texas Department of Public Safety
Austin, Texas
and
Inspector Roger Leathers
Texas Department of Public Safety
Austin, Texas

Chief Kinkland
Chief of Police
Reno Police Department
Reno, Nevada

Sheriff Doyne Bailey
Travis County Sheriff
Austin, Texas
and
Lieutenant Richard Gruetzner
Information Services
Travis County Sheriff
Austin, Texas

Officer F. A. Stewart
Highway Patrol
Arizona Department of Public Safety

Chief Drew Diamond
Chief of Police

Oklahoma Police Department
Tulsa, Oklahoma
   and
Corporal Julie Harris
Oklahoma Police Department
Tulsa, Oklahoma

E. J. Barbee
Chief of Police
Columbia Police Department
Columbia, Missouri
   and
Linda J. Calvert
Records Supervisor
Columbia Police Department
Columbia, Missouri

Chief Richard Shaffer
Bureau of Police
Harrisburg, Pennsylvania
   and
Lieutenant Richard H. King
Bureau of Police
Harrisburg, Pennsylvania

INTERNATIONAL LAW ENFORCEMENT AGENCIES

Superintendent J. Kitchen
City of London Police
London, England

Chief Constable W. T. Marshall
Vancouver Police Department
Vancouver, British Columbia
Canada
   and
Corporal D. A. LePard
Planning and Research Section

Vancouver Police Department
Vancouver, British Columbia
Canada

H. A. Jenkins
Chief Constable
West Vancouver Police Department
West Vancouver, British Columbia
Canada

B. G. Scott
Chief of Police
Brandon City Police
Brandon, Manitoba

We are also indebted to our editor, Kim Davies, for her support and encouragment.
Our first edition copy editor, Ginny Carroll, was invaluably helpful in making our
efforts understandable. Finally, we thank our families for their support, love, and
understanding during this project.

WRITTEN AND INTERPERSONAL COMMUNICATION METHODS FOR LAW ENFORCEMENT

1

The Need for Effective Communication

Outline

We take communication for granted. Reading this text is a form of communication. Taking a written examination on the text material is another form. Asking a friend to go for a cup of coffee after class is a third. All of these examples have the goal of transferring an idea from one location to another. One authority has noted that 70 percent of our time is spent communicating.[1] But even with its prominence in everyday functions, there is very little, if any, study of communication techniques required in high schools, colleges, or police academies. This chapter provides an overview of the role of oral and written communication in a law enforcement agency, and explains some of the dynamics of communicating with others.

INTRODUCTION

Is It Really Necessary to Study Report Writing?

The following excerpts are from actual police reports, many of which were sergeant approved.

> Prieto threatened that Bach was going to hers and the police were going to charged also.
>
> They put the victim on a heart monitor and received a negative heatbeat.
>
> Capt. Crane showed me the locatioon of the victim's location.
>
> Rp said the victim was pronunced dead by himself at 0200 hrs today.
>
> The rear driver's side tire was flat but I could not find an entry or exit wound through the tire.

Not only do some police officers have difficulty writing a simple sentence, their spelling can cause laughter or professional embarrassment. Some words taken from actual police reports follow:

REPORT/INTERPRETATION	REPORT/INTERPRETATION
Wipelash/Whiplash	Hart/Heart
Aroda/Aorta	Pregnate/Pregnant
Trouma/Trauma	Stapping/Stabbing
Decease/Disease	

Source: Sgt. Pie, "Police Stories Unabashed . . . and Unedited," *The Kopout* (Nov./Dec. 1991), 10.

As the preceding focus indicates, report writing—and, therefore, spelling—is a major part of any law enforcement officer's duties. Those reports are read by fellow officers, supervisors, and other professionals in the field. If you have not yet mastered the English language and spelling, now is the time to start. As a professional, you will be using them for the rest of your career.

This text, and, specifically, this chapter, reviews the importance of communication in a law enforcement environment. Simply reading and understanding this material will not make you a more effective communicator. All of us can improve our ability to communicate, either orally or in writing. However, it takes constant attention and hard work. This chapter sets forth certain basic principles that apply to all forms of communication and explains why police officers must be able to communicate appropriately in many different situations.

THE IMPORTANCE OF COMMUNICATION

Communication, oral or written, is especially critical in a law enforcement agency. The mission of any police department is to apprehend violators of the law. However, that is only the first step in the criminal justice system. Once a suspect has been arrested, a series of steps and occurrences follows: booking; follow-up investigations; submission of arrest information to local, state, and national databases; and, finally, testifying in court regarding the arrest. Police departments must also be able to communicate internally regarding procedures and policies that affect their operation. And the ability of law enforcement officers to communicate externally to groups or individuals within the community is equally important.

Communication within a Law Enforcement Environment

This text emphasizes report writing as the major form of communication within a police agency. However, it should be obvious that several different types of writing skills must be mastered by rookies as well as law enforcement administrators. Arrest reports, follow-up investigations, memorandums, standard operating procedures, and promotion tests are a few common forms of writing involved in the day-to-day operation of a police department.

Report writing is not the only form of information transfer within a law enforcement agency. Oral communication is equally important in many situations. Oral expression covers the entire spectrum of the communication process. It starts when officers greet each other before roll call, and continues through roll call and out onto the streets. Chapter 2 discusses the oral communication process in more detail.

All officers, from the least experienced to the chief, must be proficient at the art of communication. This includes the ability to express oneself orally or in writing. The new officer must understand how to communicate with citizens, fellow officers, and superiors. The sergeant must be able to transmit orders to subordinates and receive commands from superiors. Even the top law enforcement administrators must have effective communication skills, whether preparing departmental policy statements, responding to the media, or defending the department's budget to elected officials.

Obviously, communication skills are critical within a law enforcement agency. These skills include the ability to read, write, and understand what is written, as well as to orally transmit and receive information. The communication process occurs both within and outside the agency. All officers must be able to communicate effectively with members of the community they serve, as discussed in the following section.

Communication within the Community

Most students have no trouble discussing classes or current events among themselves in an informal environment. However, many of those same students become paralyzed with fear at the thought of standing up in class to explain a theory or position. The ability to communicate in public forums is an important aspect of law enforcement. Community support and police involvement in the community are critical aspects of any successful law enforcement program.[2] Other chapters address specific techniques that allow law enforcement officers to effectively transmit important information within the community. The purpose of this section is to introduce students to the concept of the community and its interaction with law enforcement.

At the local or municipal level, the chief of police is usually appointed by either the city manager or mayor. The city manager serves at the pleasure of the mayor or council, and that group of local elected officials reacts to pressure from the community. In most jurisdictions, the sheriff is elected by citizens of the county. Therefore, the sheriff will be interested in staying in touch with members of the community. Additionally, the concept of community policing is sweeping the nation, and many agencies are looking to form partnerships with local communities to battle crime. All of these factors make it imperative that law enforcement officers understand how to communicate effectively with the population of any municipality.

This communication takes different forms and works on many levels. The most basic involves one-on-one communication between an officer and a citizen. The citizen may be a victim, a witness, or a perpetrator. The dynamics of this type of communication will obviously vary depending on the status of the citizen.

Another common form of communication within the community involves officers speaking before local groups. These may include school groups, service clubs, constituents of local elected officials, and college classes. In these settings the officer provides information to the various groups.

Law enforcement officers also pass on information within the community through the local media. This form of communication reaches a very large audience and in some situations is instantaneous, as in the case of a live newscast.

There are many other forms of communication in our society. It is critical that all members of law enforcement agencies recognize the need to perfect their skills and be prepared to communicate on a variety of levels.

WRITTEN COMMUNICATION TECHNIQUES

This section is included here to allow students to start using these rules and techniques immediately. An understanding of the English language and basic grammar is a necessity in law enforcement. Unfortunately, colleges, universities, and police academies assume that all students can write at a basic, understandable level. Specific English grammar courses may be required in various institutions, but like any learned ability, unless writing is practiced, the skill achieved soon lapses. This text is not a grammar or English language book. However, certain basic rules, if learned, memorized, and used, will help police officers avoid mistakes in report writing. At the end of each chapter is a more comprehensive guide to writing. Some of the more basic techniques are discussed here.

Capitalization[3]

In effect, capitals highlight a word and point out its prominence. Rather than attempt to memorize the complex rules involved in capitalization, it is more effective to understand a few general principles underlying the capitalization of words:

1. First words of any sentence and direct quotes are capitalized.

   This officer approached the suspect.
   The suspect stated, "I didn't do it."

2. Specific places and regions are capitalized.

New York   Chicago   San Francisco
the North   Lake Superior   Hawaiian Islands
a city   to fly north   a lake   an island

3. Organizations and their members are capitalized.

Charleston Police Department   Catholics

4. Groups, races, and nationalities are capitalized.

African-American   Hispanic   Caucasian

5. Days, months, and holidays are capitalized.

Monday   June   New Year's

Frequently Confused Words[4]

There are many words in the English language that are confusing, especially those that sound alike.

1. *Accept* and *except.*

Accept means to receive or to give approval.
Except means to exclude or to leave out an item.

2. *All right* and *alright.*

All right is correct, *alright* is wrong.

3. *Affect* and *effect.*

Affect means to influence.
Effect means to bring about (verb) or a result (noun).
We want to *affect* a major change.
What was the principal *effect* of LEAA?

4. *Among* and *between.*

Among is used with three or more.
Between is used with two.
The loot was split *among* the twelve thieves.
The loot was split *between* the two thieves.

5. *Amount* and *number.*

Amount is used for things that cannot be counted.
Number is used for things that can be counted.

The *amount* of work left at the crime scene was enormous.

The *number* of dead bodies keeps increasing.

6. *Credible* and *Creditable.*

   Credible means believable.

   Creditable means reputable.

7. *Disinterested* and *uninterested.*

   Disinterested means free from selfish motives.

   Uninterested means not interested or unconcerned.

8. *Eminent* and *imminent.*

   Eminent means something that is well known.

   Imminent means something is about to happen.

9. *Farther* and *further.*

   Farther is used when speaking of distance.

   Further is used when referring to extent or degree.

10. *In* and *into.*

    In means and is used to signify a place.

    Into means and signifies an action.

    The document is *in* the safe.

    The suspect went *into* the house.

11. *Infer* and *imply.*

    Infer means to conclude.

    Imply means to suggest.

    I *infer* from the report that we need additional officers.

    Do you mean to *imply* that the butler did it?

12. *Its* and *It's.*

    Its is a possessive pronoun.

    It's is a contraction of *it is.*

    The food lost *its* flavor.

    It's a hectic holiday schedule.

13. *Lie* and *lay.*

    Lie means to be at rest or inactive.

    Lay means to place something.

    Please *lie* down until you feel better.

    Please *lay* the weapon on the bench.

14. *Your* and *you're.*

> *Your* means *of* or relating to you.
> *You're* is a contraction of *you are.*
> Is this *your* report?
> *You're* spending too much time in your patrol vehicle.

Words That Can Be Left Out[5]

1. *There,* unless it's the subject, can usually be left out.

> *Weak:* There will be three officers attending the opening.
> *Better:* Three officers will be attending the opening.

2. *That, which,* and *who* can be left out unless a misunderstanding would result.

> *Weak:* The sergeant thinks that shorter sentences are more effective.
> *Better:* The sergeant thinks shorter sentences are more effective.
> *Weak:* The union agreement which we signed runs for five years.
> *Better:* The union agreement we signed runs for five years.
> *Weak:* Mary Smith, who is my neighbor, saw the crime.
> *Better:* Mary Smith, my neighbor, saw the crime.

Intensives[6]

Can a person be a little dead? The answer is *no.* Some words should not be intensified. Adding intensive words can cause embarrassment in a courtroom.

1. Do not overuse the word *very.*

> *Weak:* It is a very impossible task.
> *Better:* It is an impossible task.

2. Be careful with the word *definitely.*

> *Weak:* That statement is definitely incorrect.
> *Better:* That statement is incorrect.

Repetition[7]

Repeating the same words shows a lack of direction. Words should be repeated only for emphasis.

1. *Each*

   Weak: Each and every

   Better: Each

2. *Foremost*

   Weak: First and foremost

   Better: Foremost

3. *Only*

   Weak: One and only

   Better: Only

4. *Total*

   Weak: Total and complete

   Better: Total

5. *Near*

   Weak: Close proximity

   Better: Near

Spelling[8]

Spelling is not a mysterious science that only selected individuals can master. It is a simple mechanical act. However, you must want to learn to spell correctly. Correct spelling takes energy and concentration. With so many other important things going on in life, correct spelling sometimes takes a low priority in our scheme of things.

Correct spelling is important for a peace officer. It saves time and embarrassment. The patrol officer doesn't like having spelling mistakes in a simple report corrected by the duty sergeant. In addition, sharp defense attorneys will be more than helpful at pointing out mistakes in a report during a jury trial. Rather than list a series of commonly misspelled words that can be memorized, the following *dos* and *don't*s of spelling are provided for review.

1. For words ending in *E* preceded by a consonant, omit the *E* before adding a suffix that begins with a vowel.

Slope	ing	Sloping
Please	ing	Pleasing
Observe	ing	Observing

2. Except for *science, I* before *E* except after *C*.

> Receive   Conceive   Perceive

3. When adding prefixes to roots, do not omit letters.

> Mis   spell   Misspell
> Over   rule   Overrule
> Room   mate   Roommate

4. There are six words that end in *-ery,* the rest end in *-ary.*

> Millinery   Confectionery   Stationery (paper)
> Monastery   Cemetery   Distillery

5. Mark every word you have to look up in the dictionary. Understand its meaning and memorize its spelling.

6. Learn how to pronounce words in order to spell them.

There are no easy rules that a police officer can adopt to avoid grammatical mistakes or misspellings. Simple concentration and hard work are the keys to success in this area of writing. The reward is less time spent redrafting simple reports and multipage documents.

SUMMARY

The ability to communicate effectively is an essential requirement for all law enforcement officers. Police officers interact with different groups on a daily basis and must be able to interact with each of them. Communication plays an important role in our personal and professional lives.

Communication involves both oral and written methods. Law enforcement personnel must be proficient in both forms of communication. Police officers must be able to communicate effectively within their agency and outside the agency to members of the community they serve. Both forms of communication are critical to a well-functioning law enforcement agency.

The old adage *practice makes perfect* is especially applicable to the communication process. Law enforcement personnel should attempt to improve their communication skills daily. Learning simple rules of capitalization and other techniques that are used in written communication will make an officer a more effective member of the agency.

REVIEW QUESTIONS

1. Which form of communication, oral or written, is most important in the following situations? Justify your answers.

   a. To the patrol officer on a beat.

   b. To the captain in charge of the Records Division.

c. To the chief.

d. To the prosecutor.

e. To the citizen who is a victim of a crime.

2. What is the key distinction between channels of information and direction of information?

3. Who should be responsible for correcting mistakes in a police report?

a. The officer who makes the mistake.

b. The officer's supervisor.

c. The prosecutor who tries the case.

4. If you were advising a young rookie on the importance of grammar and spelling and could state only one rule, what would it be?

PRACTICAL APPLICATIONS

1. If you discovered a mistake in grammar in your sergeant's report, how would you handle the situation?

a. If the sergeant was your supervisor.

b. If the sergeant was a peer.

c. If you supervised the sergeant.

2. Review a classmate's notes from another class. Do these notes give you a clear picture of what occurred in the class? List your reasons and see if the classmate agrees with you.

3. Take turns spelling the Words to Know listed at the end of each chapter with a classmate and then check each other's spelling of the same words. What are the most commonly misspelled words? Why do you think they are so often misspelled?

4. In each of the rows below, circle the correctly spelled word:

abandon	abandan	abondon	abonden
abaord	abord	aboard	aboarde
absenca	absence	absenc	absance
backward	bardward	backard	backword
bialliff	bailliff	bailiff	balift
barbiturate	barbutrate	bardutirade	barbiturete
cafeteria	cafteria	cafetiria	cafetiria
calcalute	calcaulate	calcarute	calculate
calendar	callander	calander	callender
damage	demage	damege	dameage

5. Rewrite the following sentences as needed:
   a. The amount of dead bodies found at the scene kept increasing.

   _____

   b. We had four dollars between the three of us.

   _____

   c. The officer excepted the package from the mailman.

   _____

   d. His conduct was designed to effect the voting patterns of hispanics.

   _____

   e. Its a cold day in june when the snow is still on the ground.

   _____

6. Define and explain the following words, concepts, or terms:
   a. communications

   _____

   b. intensives

   _____

   c. dynamics of communicating

   _____

   d. external communications

   _____

   e. report writing

   _____

7. The following paragraph was taken from an actual police report. Make it a better paragraph.

   This officer responded to the location of the parking lot of Von's and upon arrival oberserved two male subjects facing each other as if they wanted to fight. This officer exited the police vehicle and upon doing so subject Wolson turned and ran eastbound through the alley. At this time this officer responded to subject Hamm who was standing at the location and this officer yelled at subject Wolson to freeze and to return to this officer.

   _____

   _____

   _____

   _____

WORDS TO KNOW

communication	records
dispatcher	spoken
oral	

ENDNOTES

1. David K. Beryl, *The Process of Communications* (New York: Holt, Rinehart, Winston, 1960).

2. John Gnagey and Ronald Henson, "Community Surveys Help Determine Police Strategies," *Police Chief* (Mar. 1995): 25.

3. See Arthur H. Bell and Roger Wyse, *The One-Minute Business Writer* (Homewood, Ill.: Dow Jones-Irwin, 1987), 128.

4. Ibid., 137.

5. See Laura Brill, *Business Writing Quick & Easy,* 2d ed. (New York: American Management Association, 1981), 12.

6. Ibid., 13.

7. Ibid., 14.

8. Bell and Wyse, *The One-Minute Business Writer,* 131.

2

Oral versus Written Communication

LEARNING OBJECTIVES

After reading this chapter, you should understand the following concepts:
• The process of communication.
• The different types of channels and directions of communication.
• The basic elements of writing.

KEY TERMS

Channels of information—The method or avenue by which information flows from one party to another.

Clarification—A request from subordinates to managers for clarification of a previous downward communication.

Communication—A process involving several steps, among two or more persons, for the primary purpose of exchanging information.

Direction of information—The way in which communication flows.

Horizontal communication—The flow of information between officers at the same organizational level.

Horizontal coordination communication—An attempt by several parties to ensure the proper order or relationship between various law enforcement functions.

Information—A form of upward communication, usually in response to a request from supervisors.

Orders—Downward communications that relate to a specific job assignment or performance.

Performance communication—Information that travels upward to police managers from subordinates to keep the managers informed regarding the subordinates' performance.

Personnel information—A broad area that covers the entire spectrum of personnel issues, from performance evaluations to authorization of overtime or leave time.

Procedures—Are intended to exist for an indefinite period of time and apply to all personnel, or to certain classes of personnel, within the department.

Upward communications—Information which travels from subordinates to managers.

Writing—A method of recording and communicating ideas by means of a system of visual marks.

Every word that you write in your report, you must be able to justify in a court of law.

—Veteran prosecutor to a rookie cop

The preceding quote is one that every officer should remember when picking up a pen or sitting down at a computer to fill out a police report. A police officer must be able to explain why the report was written as filed, justify any omissions, and testify from the contents of that report in a court of law. Testifying in court combines both written and oral communication skills. However, that is only a small part of a law enforcement officer's duties. A professional must master these skills to effectively carry out the diverse duties that are encountered by officers in any modern police agency.

Oral communication skills are necessary to talk with members of the general public, request assistance from other officers, advise suspects of their *Miranda rights,* and inform supervisors that certain actions have occurred. In addition, oral skills are needed to understand and transmit statements made by citizens, suspects, and superiors.

Written communication skills are required to fill out various police reports, draft narrative summaries, and understand written policy directives.[1] Written reports are the basis for recalling past events, and police officers rely on them daily when they testify in court. The ability to write in a clear, concise, and understandable manner does not come naturally. Like any activity, it must be practiced until it is mastered. Once mastered, those skills must continually be used or they will become unfocused and useless. A professional athlete spends hours each day honing the skills necessary to participate in a sport. However, police officers may spend less than 10 percent of any shift writing reports regarding their activity.

All police officers, from rookies to chiefs, must be able to speak, listen, write, and understand. The ability to effectively communicate orally does not do away with the necessity of writing. Conversely, effective writing does not do away with the requirement of good oral communication skills. These skills are intertwined and dependent on each other. Any effective police officer will acquire, maintain, and continually sharpen both skills. Oral communication is the foundation on which written skills are built.

ORAL COMMUNICATION

Talking and listening are skills we learn at an early age. As we progress through school, these skills are sharpened under pain of failing classes. When formal schooling is finished, the police academy is behind us, and we are sworn officers on the street, we find ourselves in a subculture that has its own formal language, customs, and traditions. Not only must we communicate within our immediate professional circle, all law enforcement officers must interact with various groups outside the police department. This requires the ability to communicate with others on many different levels.

Communication Defined

The communication process is both a simple and complex series of events. To properly understand this process we must agree on a definition of the term *communication*. One text states that there are at least 94 different definitions of communication.[2] Depending on which definition you choose, it encompasses the following elements:

1. It is a process, rather than an isolated event.
2. It involves at least two persons.
3. The primary purpose is the exchange of information.

Communication can then be defined as a process involving several steps, between two or more persons, for the primary purpose of exchanging information. The following sections discuss this process and explain the different directions or channels through which information is processed.

How the Process Occurs

This section examines how the process of communication takes place and explains the three elements of the communication process. The act of communicating a thought or idea to another person is not an isolated event; it is a process and involves more than one step.

It Is a Process Rather Than an Isolated Event Some authorities believe there are as many as seven distinct steps in the communication process.[3] However, for purposes of simplicity, we will break down the flow of information into five basic steps. Communication requires (1) the transmission of an idea, (2) sending that idea via a medium, (3) receipt of the message, (4) understanding the idea, and (5) feedback to the sender of the message. If there is a failure in any of these five steps, the communication process is flawed and information will not flow in a smooth, accurate manner.

The transmission of an idea This step implies the formation of a thought or thoughts and the desire to express those ideas. Every day we have thoughts that are better left unsaid, but we go ahead and act on them—even though it might be inappropriate to express those thoughts, or the reason for our actions, to another.

For example, a fellow officer might have a bad body odor. In such situations we might express our feelings, either in a joking manner or otherwise: "Boy, I can tell you love garlic on your bread, I can still smell it this morning. Why didn't you bring me some?" This kind of message, coupled with the act of moving away from your partner, is an expression that has been transmitted and acted on.

On the other hand, you might simply move away and not express any offense if the person is unknown to you or you are uncomfortable communicating sensitive thoughts or ideas. Therefore, to communicate, an idea must be formed and an intentional act must take place to transmit that idea to another person.

Sending an idea via a medium Once a message is formed it must be sent. There are many ways to transmit ideas: orally, in writing, or by action. Everyone understands the difference between an oral reprimand and a written reprimand that is made a permanent part of an officer's personnel file. The same information can be conveyed by either medium; however, a written reprimand is considered more grave than an oral one. By the same token, written memorandums are more formal and more serious than oral directions. Even verbal communications have many variations, and the tone of voice may have a dramatic impact. "I would like you to leave" can be a soft-spoken, friendly request, or it can be shouted and delivered as an order. Thus, the medium, the method by which the idea is transmitted, will determine how it is received and acted on.

Receipt of the message Drafting a memorandum or standard operating procedure without distributing it to department personnel does not accomplish anything. In addition, the memorandum or standard operating procedure (SOP) must be understood by the parties it affects. Thus, receipt of the message is a critical step in the communication process. It is the reverse of the transmission of a message in that the message must be received and acted on to be effective.

Understanding the idea Transmitting a message is useless unless someone comprehends its content. Since this step occurs prior to any feedback, the sender should attempt to place himself in the receiving party's position and frame the message so that the essence of the idea is communicated. It is therefore critical that the message be clear and easily understood by the receiving party.

Feedback to the sender of the message This is the last step in the communication process, where the communication loop is closed. By this we mean that the sender receives data indicating that the message was understood or needs clarification.

Let's return to the example of a departmental standard operating procedure. Normally, many such documents are circulated in draft form for review and comment. The affected divisions in the department comment on the impact of the SOP on their operations and suggest any changes that would improve their own operations or would assist in carrying out the objective of the SOP. The division officer responsible for submitting the final draft of the document to the chief for signature then makes any necessary changes to the SOP, based on the other divisions' comments. This is an example of feedback in a formal setting.

Feedback may also occur verbally, with one partner telling another, "I don't understand what you want me to do"; or by actions, such as a quizzical look or a shrug of the shoulders. No matter what form feedback takes, its purpose is to acknowledge the receipt of the message, clarify the contents of the message, or indicate some response to the message.

Feedback will be discussed in more detail later in this chapter.

Communication Involves at Least Two Persons Communication does not occur in a vacuum. The desire or motivation to express ideas, thoughts, and feelings is based on the need for expression from one person to another. Sure, many of us talk to ourselves at times, whether an expletive when we hit our thumb with a hammer or a simple question to ourselves, like "How could I have been so stupid?" The purpose of these statements is not to convey information to another; rather, they are rhetorical or reactive types of utterances. The purpose of communication is the expression or transmission of data. However, communication is not limited to one-on-one situations. We communicate to individuals or groups and, in some cases, to the general public. A patrol officer may well face all of these situations during the course of one day.

The officer may start the day in roll-call training by asking the patrol sergeant about the condition of a new stop sign at an intersection on her beat. This is one-on-one communication. Later, during the shift, she may address a crowd of citizens at the scene of an accident, requesting that they move out of the way of the emergency vehicle. This is communication with a group. Finally, she may describe the accident for *Action News* on television. This is communication with the general public. All of these examples reinforce the principle that communication involves the transmission of data to someone else.

The Primary Purpose Is the Exchange of Information Most of the time, we do not act without some known or unknown objective. While patrol officers may engage in small talk to pass the early morning hours on a stakeout, even this type of communication serves a need: it may indeed be for no other purpose than to pass the time and keep each officer alert, it may be a necessary ingredient in the formation or maintenance of a professional association or friendship, or it may serve some other purpose.

This transfer of information also occurs at a formal level. For example, it might be a new departmental directive regarding the use of force that each officer is required to sign after reading, or it might be a roll-call briefing on the modus operandi of a serial rapist. Information is also exchanged at an informal level, such as a discussion between two officers over a cup of coffee regarding which type of handgun is the best weapon to carry while off duty.

Channels and Directions

Channels and *directions* of communication deal with the flow or movement of information from the sender to the recipient. *Channel* refers to the method or avenue by which information flows from one party to another, and *direction* indicates just that—which way the communication flows.

There are two communication channels in any organization. The traditional route or method of communication in any police organization usually follows the chain of command. This type of communication channel is typified by formal orders, directives, and written memorandums. These forms of communication provide a sense of order and security to a police organization. However, there are several disadvantages to the excessive or exclusive use of formal communications within a law enforcement agency. Strict adherence to formal channels of communication is a time- and personnel-consuming effort. The memorandums must be carefully drafted, endorsed via the chain of command, and forwarded to the addressee pursuant to departmental policy. The second major drawback with formal channels of communication is the effect they have on the free flow of information. Their very rigidity restricts spontaneous ideas and thought. Formal routes usually require a written record—this by itself may restrict the flow of information, since many people are hesitant to place their thoughts or ideas in writing. A fourth disadvantage is the inability to respond to changing situations rapidly. Formal channels are by their very nature rigid, and any change or modification must be reviewed and staffed within those very same channels. If new situations arise, the modification process may not be able to keep pace with the need for change.

Considering all of these disadvantages, one might question the need for formal channels of communication. However, they provide certain advantages to any organization and to law enforcement agencies specifically. Formal communication ensures that all officers within the department receive the same information. This is critical when new directives are formulated or when information concerning certain crimes needs to be passed to all officers on patrol. Formal communication is usually more concise and clear than informal methods, and there is less confusion regarding the purpose or content of the message. Also, formality provides for uniformity—all personnel receive the same information at the same time. Finally, formal communication establishes a paper trail for purposes of court hearings. Formal communication channels are a fact of life in any large organization. With its emphasis on court hearings and testimony, the need for this type of communication in a law enforcement agency is critical.

However, total reliance on formal communication channels can also be detrimental to the effective operation of a police department. Informal channels are the unofficial routes of communication within a law enforcement agency—that is, the grapevine or departmental gossip. These channels do not appear on any table of organization and they may not be officially sanctioned by the department. But they are a fact of life. A police department is a notorious rumor mill regarding what goes on within the department. However, informal channels of communication do more than serve as a conduit for idle gossip—they provide a needed link within the organization.

Most formal channels of communication flow from the top of an organization to the bottom. Very few police departments provide for formal communication *across* the organization. Informal channels of communication provide this necessary linkage.

There are a number of situations in which informal channels are utilized within a department. One of the most common is the interaction between detectives and patrol officers. At times, detectives approach patrol officers to ask for clarification of an initial report. Conversely, a patrol officer may remember something about a crime scene that was not recorded and go back to the detective assigned to the case to discuss the matter and determine if a follow-up report detailing the additional fact should be submitted to the detective's sergeant.

When time is a critical factor, informal channels are utilized. The formal channel would require the information to go up the chain of command and back down to the intended recipient. This is time consuming. Utilizing informal channels, the officer can cut across lines of authority and responsibility to pass the information quickly.

Informal communication channels are also used in situations when two sections or divisions need to cooperate on a case or a series of crimes. Robbery and homicide divisions may find themselves in this situation when a robbery victim is killed. The robbery division might have information that would assist the homicide detective in solving the crime.

Because informal channels of communication provide an alternative method of receiving information, senior law enforcement officials should not attempt to extinguish them. Rather, they should allow them to exist in a form that enhances the effectiveness of the organization. Some scholars have suggested that formal and informal channels of communication be blended into one communications network that is responsive to the department's goals.[4]

Formal and informal channels of communication provide the means or avenues for the movement of information within a police department. These are the highways and back roads on which information moves from one point to another. The formal channels are similar to highways—they are well known, clearly marked, and occasionally congested with traffic. The informal channels are sometimes known only to the locals—they twist and turn and often encounter detours and other roadblocks.

While channels of communication explain *how* information moves in an organization, they do not explain the different *directions* in which information travels. Information may travel in any number of directions within an organization, but the most common movements are upward, downward, and horizontal.[5] The remaining portion of this section will examine the directions of communication flow within a law enforcement agency.

The most obvious directions of information flow in any organization are upward and downward. This is traditionally the chain of command, and it coincides with the formal channels of communication. Downward communication is usually classified into three broad categories: (1) orders, (2) procedures, and (3) personnel information.

Orders are downward communications that relate to a specific job assignment or performance. An example is the patrol listing that assigns officers to various beats, shifts, and work days. Orders are specific and usually related to a short period of time. They are directed at individual officers rather than the department as a whole.

Procedures are a second form of downward communication directed to a broad subject. Departmental standard operating procedures are an example of information that flows from the top to the bottom of an organization along the formal channels of communication. SOPs are intended to exist for an indefinite period of time and apply to all personnel or to certain classes of personnel within the department.

Personnel information is the third category of downward information. This is a broad area that covers the entire spectrum of personnel issues from performance evaluations to authorizations to work overtime or take leave. In many instances, this type of information has a substantial impact on the morale of the department. This type of downward communication directly impacts the personal lives of officers and their families.

These three types of downward communication are critical to management's ability to direct the department. However, the second direction of communication, upward communication, is just as important to the healthy function of a law enforcement agency. Upward communication is information from subordinates that travels from the bottom of the department to its managers. This type of communication may be broken down into three major categories: (1) performance, (2) information, and (3) clarification.

Performance communication is information that travels upward from subordinates to police managers and keeps the managers informed regarding the performance of their subordinates. This information could be statistics gathered by the patrol sergeant on the number of arrests made during each shift or complaints by individual officers regarding working conditions. This form of upward communication may go through either formal or informal channels, but is more likely to take place through formal channels, in the form of reports on the performance of certain divisions or sections.

Information is a form of upward communication that is usually a response to a request from supervisors. For example, a draft SOP on record filing is distributed to certain patrol sergeants by the lieutenant of records. Accompanying this is a request that the documents be reviewed from a patrol perspective and any comments for possible changes to the draft forwarded back. This type of upward communication usually flows through the formal channels of a department, since it is a type of formalized feedback.

Clarification is the final form of upward communication. As its name implies, it is a request from subordinates to managers for clarification of a previous downward communication. Similar to the upward flow of information, this usually occurs within the formal channels of a law enforcement department. For example, an upward request for clarification could deal with a new directive regarding the number of leave days officers are authorized during official holidays. Does the holiday count against an officer's leave if it falls on a normal day off, or must they work even if they have requested vacation, and so on. Unfortunately, many police agencies' personnel directives are unclear, and officers or their immediate supervisors will request either an oral interpretation or written guidance to explain the broad policy statement in the directive. Upward communication serves a critical function in a law enforcement agency. It provides police supervisors with a form of feedback that can assist them in performing their duties.

The third and final direction that communications may take is *horizontal.* Horizontal communication is the flow of information between officers at the same organizational level. This type of communication provides a necessary link between officers and divisions within the department. Horizontal communication may be classified into three categories: (1) coordination, (2) social issues, and (3) problem solving.

Horizontal *coordination* communication is an attempt by the parties to ensure there is a proper order or relationship between various law enforcement functions. This type of communication is concerned with the proper performance of various tasks. For example, the robbery detail needs to coordinate with the patrol units in the area when planning to stake out a store that they believe may be hit in the near future.

Social issues are critical in any police organization. Horizontal communication is used by individual officers to contact their peers and friends in the department. This communication may run the spectrum from an invitation to have a beer after the shift to the imposition of social expectations on fellow officers by passing the word that Officer X was seen at a local bar and had to be driven home by a friend.

The final form of horizontal communication concerns the ability of peers to discuss and *solve common problems.* All of us are reluctant to reinvent the wheel. If someone has already come up with a solution that works, for the most part we will readily adopt such an approach. Peace officers are no different. An officer who is confronted with a problem will discuss that issue with peers in an effort to find out if someone else has faced the issue and how they solved it.

The channels and directions that communication takes are important in understanding how information moves from the sender to the receiver. Formal channels of communication are the easiest to recognize because they traditionally follow the chain of command. However, the informal channels of communication provide a necessary link within any organization. Communications may move in any number of directions, the most common being downward, upward, and horizontal. This network of information on lines within an organization provides the glue that holds it together in good times and bad.

Communications and Courtesy

Courtesy to citizens is an important part of any law enforcement officer's duties. We express ourselves in a number of ways, and the way officers express themselves to citizens is an extremely important aspect of the law enforcement profession.

Simple guidelines follow that address the most common applications of courtesy and communication in law enforcement:

1. *Introductions.* Whenever practical, all officers should identify themselves by title and name at the start of any contact with a citizen. The simple use of common greetings such as "Good morning" or "Good afternoon" can go a long way toward setting the tone of any encounter.
2. *Tone of voice.* Speech is the primary communication tool used by law enforcement officers. Officers should always be aware of their voice tone and use it to their advantage. The voice should never betray anger, contempt, sarcasm, or other inflections that are likely to provoke opposition.
3. *Forms of address.* Officers should not address citizens by their first names unless the circumstances clearly make it appropriate.
4. *Body language.* While officers must often assume stances that are required to preserve safety during encounters with the public, care must be taken to avoid mannerisms that needlessly provoke negative reactions from citizens. Resting a hand on the butt of a weapon is one example of such behavior.
5. *Profanity.* The use of profanity is never appropriate.
6. *Demeaning remarks.* Any form of address that ridicules a citizen or expresses contempt is never appropriate.
7. *Explaining what we do.* The most simple form of courtesy and communication is explaining what we are doing and why.

Source: Adapted from Thomas J. Lange, "Cultivating the Practice of Courtesy," The Police Chief (Jan. 1989): 35.

This section has discussed the concept of oral communication and defined that term. We have examined how communication is processed, and have reviewed how it travels from one person or place to another. However, this is just the beginning of understanding communication in a police agency. Another aspect of communication is the written word.

WRITTEN COMMUNICATION

Introduction

Voltaire used to read to his cook everything he wrote. If she could not understand it, he would rewrite it.[6] If one of the world's most famous philosophers could rewrite his works in an effort to make them more understandable, so can any law enforcement officer. One of the main problems with written communication is the lack of instant feedback. Oral communication is interactive and allows for almost instantaneous correction by using feedback to clarify any misunderstanding. Written communication does not provide this mechanism. If a report, memorandum, or directive is ambiguous, that fact must be transmitted to the writer after the document has been placed in circulation. Because of this lack of instantaneous feedback, written communication takes more effort than oral communication.

Records and record keeping occupy a critical place in any law enforcement agency. Without the ability to communicate in writing, any police department would be crippled. Arrest reports, follow-up reports, departmental directives, and budget documents are just a few examples of necessary written statements that are present in any police agency—large or small.

Writing Defined

The term *writing* has many definitions. This text deals with a specialized form of writing—report writing for law enforcement professionals. Based on the scope of this text, writing may be defined as *a method of recording and communicating ideas by means of a system of visual marks*. This definition has three basic elements:

1. *A recording of ideas.* Writing is lasting. It is a permanent form of communication. The spoken word is gone from our senses as soon as it ends, whereas writing is a permanent record of our thoughts and ideas. It may be reviewed 10 days or 10 years after it is transmitted.
2. *A method of communication.* The preceding section explained the process of communication. One of the distinctions between oral and written communication is the lack of instant feedback that allows the person transmitting the data to correct, refine, or focus the information into a more understandable format.
3. *It involves a system of visual marks.* Writing used to be confined to printed or cursive matter. If our printing or handwriting was illegible, others had to struggle to interpret it. However, they could rely on the fact that we were using known and accepted words to find the meaning of our printed or written message. In this day of computers, certain symbols have taken on new meanings. The symbol *C:* has an accepted meaning for anyone who uses computers.

Similarly, *.* carries a distinct meaning. In police work, numbers are just as important. Depending on the jurisdiction, a certain collection of numbers connotates a crime. *P.C. 459* indicates a burglary in California. These numbers are usually shorthand for the criminal statute defining the crime. In California Penal Code Section 459, the elements of burglary are listed. Each jurisdiction will have its own set of numbers that are recognizable to its police officers. These numbers may be shorthand for crimes, specialized codes used over the radio, or other law-enforcement-related activities that have by custom or practice become known by a string of numbers.

Writing police reports is no easy task. Nor can any one test deal with the many forms and procedures used by the various law enforcement agencies in the United States or the world. However, a few simple guidelines may help any law enforcement officer when he or she first begins to draft police reports.

SUMMARY

Up to 70 percent of our time is spent communicating with others. Communication is a process involving several steps, among two or more persons, for the primary purpose of exchanging information. This process requires sending an idea, receipt of that idea by the other party, understanding the idea, and feedback to the sender of the message.

Information moves through various channels and directions. In most police departments, formal channels of communication follow the chain of command. This has several advantages and disadvantages. Informal channels of communication also exist in all law enforcement agencies. These informal channels should be utilized to upgrade the flow of information within the department.

Written communication is harder to master than oral communication because there is a lack of instant feedback when written communication is utilized. Police reports form the basis for future action in the criminal justice system. Prosecutors rely on them when issuing criminal complaints. Officers will refer to them to refresh their memories when testifying in court. Probation officers may review them when deciding what form of punishment the accused should receive.

There is no simple method by which a police officer becomes an experienced writer. Practice, hard work, and attention to detail are the key ingredients of a successfully drafted police report.

REVIEW QUESTIONS

1. What is more important—oral or written communication? Why? Justify your answer.

2. If you could use only one channel of information in an agency, which one would it be?

3. Based on your reading to this point, what is the purpose of a written report? How is it different from an oral report?

4. Why is it important to improve our communication skills?

5. What are the chief differences between oral and written communication?

BETTER WRITING DRILLS

Law enforcement officers are often required to use nouns and/or adjectives that describe a suspect, witness, or victim's nationality. The following chart lists a country or region with the noun and adjective for that country. Look at the country and attempt to spell the noun and/or adjective for that country correctly. Check your results in the accompanying boxes.

COUNTRY OR REGION	NOUN	ADJECTIVE
Afghanistan	Afghan(s)	Afghan
Argentina	Argentine(s)	Argentine
Australia	Australian(s)	Australian
Bangladesh	Bangladeshi(s)	Bangladesh
Belgium	Belgian(s)	Belgian
Brazil	Brazilian(s)	Brazilian
Canada	Canadian(s)	Canadian
Colombia	Colombian(s)	Colombian
Cuba	Cuban(s)	Cuban
Denmark	Dane(s)	Danish
El Salvador	Salvadoran(s)	Salvadoran
Haiti	Haitian(s)	Haitian
Laos	Lao or Laotian(s)	Lao or Laotian
Mexico	Mexican(s)	Mexican
Philippines	Filipino(s)	Philippine
Spain	Spaniard(s)	Spanish
Taiwan	Chinese	Chinese
Thailand	Thai	Thai
United Kingdom	Briton or British	British
Vietnam	Vietnamese	Vietnamese

PRACTICAL APPLICATIONS

1. The most effective way to improve your writing is to do freewriting exercises regularly, at least twice a week. These exercises are sometimes called "babbling" exercises. The idea is to write for at least 10 minutes without stopping. Never look back, and do not stop to correct spelling or to think about what you are doing. The only requirement in the exercise is never to stop writing until time has expired. During this semester, do one freewriting exercise regarding any subject before each class. At the end of the semester compare your earlier freewriting exercises with your later ones. You should notice an improvement in your writing ability.

2. Punctuate the following sentence:

   Woman without her man is a savage.[7]

   Compare your punctuation with that of your classmates. Does punctuation change the meaning of the sentence?[7]

3. In each of the rows below, circle the correctly spelled word:

abutement	abuttment	abutment	abuttement
accessible	acessible	acessibile	accessibile
beligerent	beligeront	belligerent	beligorent
bactera	bacteria	bacterria	baterria
cartilage	cortilage	cartolige	cartilag
conscientious	consceintious	consceintous	conscientous
dupilicate	duplicat	duplicate	duplecate
evaise	evasive	eavaise	evsiave
gurdian	guardian	guardin	gaurdian
homice	homicide	homcide	homcidi

4. Rewrite the following sentences as needed:

   a. He saw the bank rounding the corner.

   _____

   b. The officer found marijuana outside the car wrapped in paper.

   _____

   c. Went to the crime scene and lost his gun.

   _____

   d. He ran quick.

   _____

e. Drinking coffee often keeps me and him awake.

_____

5. Define and explain the following words or terms:

   a. performance communications

   _____

   b. upward communications

   _____

   c. horizontal communications

   _____

   d. direction of information

   _____

   e. channels of information

   _____

6. The following paragraph was taken from an actual police report. Make it a better paragraph:

   At this point, this officer asked subject Hamm what transpired and the subject simply did not answer this officer. It should be noted that at this time Officer Smith arrived and the scence and while this officer was briefing Officer Smith the subjects were once again facing each other and at this time this officer heard subject Hamm state "Okay you still want to fitgh. At this time the officer stepped among the subjects and drawed his baton from the baton ring and ordering the subjects to go to the rear of the vehicle.

   _____

   _____

   _____

   _____

   _____

WORDS TO KNOW

accuracy	carefully
acquaintance	ceiling
aggravated	communication
burglary	conscious

description	license
eliminate	management
February	miscellaneous
government	pamphlet
homicide	realize
inadequate	refuse

ENDNOTES

1. Michael T. D'Aulizio and Kathy M. Sheehan, "Instituting Quality Control Measures for Police Reports," *The Police Chief* (Oct. 1992): 129.

2. Harry W. More and W. Fred Wegener, *Effective Police Supervision* (Cincinnati, Ohio: Anderson, 1990), 38.

3. See R. C. Huseman, *Interpersonal Communication: A Guide for Staff Development* (Athens, Ga.: Institute of Government, University of Georgia, Aug. 1974).

4. Bernard Beryls and Gary A. Steiner, *Human Behavior: An Inventory of Scientific Findings* (New York: Harcourt, Brace & World, 1964), 370.

5. See Anthony Davis, *Inside Bureaucracy* (Boston: Little, Brown, 1967), 235–247.

6. Voltaire (1694–1778) was a famous French writer and philosopher. He traveled throughout Europe and penned numerous treaties, poems, and articles. Considered one of the most prolific writers of that period, his works contain memorable passages distinguished by elegance, perspicuity, and wit. One of his most famous essays was "The Henriad" (1728).

7. One English professor directed her students to punctuate this sentence correctly. One male student wrote: "Woman, without her man, is a savage." A female student wrote: "Woman! Without her, man is a savage."

3

The Communication Process

After reading this chapter, you should understand the following concepts:
• How the Johari window model of communication works.
• The different models Schramm developed to explain the communication process.
• How Lasswell viewed communication.
• The difference between individual and group communication.

KEY TERMS

Centrality of communication—The degree of centralization of the message flow and decision making.

Communications network—The pattern of information that flows among members of a group.

Decoder—The process by which symbols are received and converted into ideas by the person receiving the information.

Encoder—The process by which ideas are converted to symbols for transmission to another person.

Group—A number of persons gathered or classified together.

Group communication—Involves interaction among three or more individuals in a face-to-face situation who share a common need that is satisfied by the exchange of information.

Interpersonal communication—The sharing of information between two persons.

Propaganda—The management of collective attitudes by the manipulation of significant symbols.

Signal—Symbols that are produced and transmitted.

Source—The brain of the person starting the communication process.

No records system can operate without clearly communicated policies, directives, and procedures. Nor can any police agency or officer carry out a mission or survive without clear communications. Communication involves more than shouting "Halt, police officer!" or ordering a patrol officer to respond to an emergency call.

This chapter examines the basic parameters of interpersonal and organization communication in a law enforcement agency. Other chapters will review special situations which involve communication issues. Chapter 2 indicated that the communication process can be both a simple and complex series of events. Communication is defined as a process involving several steps, among two or more persons, for the primary purpose of exchanging information. The dynamics of communication, or how we react to information, is an important aspect of the communication cycle. The next section reviews the interaction between a person who sends a message and the way in which the receiver processes that information.

THE JOHARI WINDOW

The preceding section pointed out how important effective communication is to a law enforcement agency generally, and a police officer, as a member of that organization, specifically. This section examines one model law enforcement officers can use to evaluate their communication skills. One of the simplest and most common communication models within law enforcement, it is known as the *Johari window.*

The Four Regions of Knowledge

Joseph Left and Harry Night created a communication model and named it after themselves. They combined their names and called the model the Johari window.[1] This model has four regions or areas that represent basic areas of knowledge or information held by the manager and others. The Johari window is illustrated here:

	Known to self	Not known to self
Known to others	Free area I	Blind area II
Not known to others	Hidden area III	Unknown area IV

The four panes or windows represent relevant information about the manager's ability to interact with other persons effectively. The Johari window has two basic aspects of communication: *exposure* and *feedback*. The *exposure* area concerns the ability of the police administrator to express feelings and ideas in an open method. This is basically the manager's ability to transmit information. The *feedback* area involves the ability of the administrator to receive information from others.

The Johari window's panes are distinct regions that encompass the following characteristics:

Area I: This pane is known as the *free area* or *arena.* It is that portion of a manager's communication ability that allows one to freely share and receive information with and from others. This ability is the key to a successful interpersonal relationship in an organization.[2] Therefore, the larger this pane or region is in relationship to the other panes, the more effective the manager becomes in dealing with superiors and subordinates.

Area II: This pane is known as the *blind area* or *blindspot.* We have all heard or used the term, "I was blindsided!" This area represents information known by others—superiors, peers, or subordinates—that is not known to the administrator. In many bureaucracies, individuals take the position that knowledge or information is power. In some ways this is true. Police officers cannot make a valid decision if information is hidden from them. The larger this pane, the more information is being withheld from the manager.

Area III: This pane is known as the *hidden area* or the *facade.* It is the area in which an officer keeps information private. Many of us make conscious or unconscious decisions to withhold certain information from others. This information may relate to personal habits or professional knowledge. When an officer withholds information, Area I, the free area or arena, is prevented from expanding. All of us withhold a portion of ourselves from others. This is only normal and healthy. The problem arises when an individual withholds information to the extent that it prevents a free, honest interchange of knowledge.

Area IV: This pane is known as the *unknown area.* It is the area that contains information that is unknown to both the manager and superiors, as well as subordinates. As the free area or arena grows through effective communication, the unknown area shrinks.

These four areas will expand or contract depending on the type of interpersonal communication patterns the manager adopts.

The Four Basic Types of Communication Patterns

The Johari window establishes four basic types of communication patterns in relation to the process of exposure and feedback. To understand how the Johari model functions, we will briefly examine each of these types.

Type A With this officer there is very little feedback or exposure. The person who is typified by this alternative does not communicate with subordinates or superiors. We have all interacted with the type of individual who withdraws from the decision-making process and is not willing to take a risk by making a decision. This officer is more concerned with self-protection than with functioning effectively. The unknown area is the dominating factor with this type of manager, while the free area or arena is correspondingly smaller.

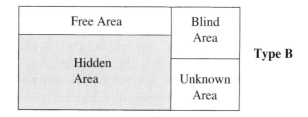

Type A

Type B This officer does not transmit information to superiors, subordinates, or peers, but will accept some interaction and feedback from them. This individual does not trust fellow officers, but must receive information from them as a survival technique. We have all encountered individuals who constantly ask for our opinions or thoughts, but are hesitant to reciprocate by telling us what they believe or feel. This officer has a large hidden area or facade in the model.

Free Area	Blind Area
Hidden Area	Unknown Area

Type B

Type C This officer is characterized by continual self-expression and refusal to accept feedback from others. In this situation, the model shows an increase in exposure with a corresponding decrease in feedback. These are the individuals whose egos are so large that they believe they have all the right answers and strive to emphasize their authority and dominance over other officers. Friends and colleagues soon come to believe that they do not value the opinions of others or will only tolerate feedback that confirms their own beliefs or position. This officer is characterized by a large blindspot in the Johari window.

Free Area	Blind Area
Hidden Area	Unknown Area

Type C

Type D This officer is considered the type of individual who shows outstanding leadership. He or she emphasizes open lines of communication, with feedback from superiors and subordinates alike. Unfortunately, many police officers are not used to dealing with this type of person and may distrust such communication techniques at first. This officer has a large free area or arena displayed in the model.

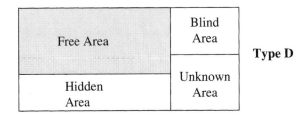

It should be obvious from the preceding discussion that the most effective law enforcement officer is Type D. This officer's relationships are characterized by trust, open lines of communication, and candor with superiors, peers, and subordinates. Open lines of communication result in a high quality of work from all the parties who interact with this type of police administrator.

The Johari window is an abstract concept that illustrates certain principles regarding the quality and style of interpersonal relationships. Its principles can be applied to any relationship; however, it is particularly applicable to law enforcement agencies. By studying and understanding the dynamics of the Johari window, we can enhance our ability to become effective law enforcement officers.

OTHER COMMUNICATION MODELS

Several other models deal with the dynamics of communication. All of these models or theories seek to explain how the communication process works. Each of these models has its advocates. It is important to understand that different respected theories examine the same process from different perspectives. Schramm and Lasswell were two of the early pioneers in the field of communications. Both of these leaders established models of communication that are still viable today.

Schramm's Model

Wilbur Schramm (1907–1987) introduced a model which illustrated the importance of interpersonal communication.[3] He is considered by many to be the father of the study of communications, and he played a critical role in the development of this research.[4] He was the first academic professional to identify himself as a communications scholar, he created the first degree in communications, and he trained the first generation of communications scholars. He founded research institutes at the University of Iowa, the University of Illinois, and Stanford, and he published numerous texts and articles dealing with the dynamics of communications.

From 1948 to 1977, Schramm produced almost a book a year dealing with the study of communications,[5] in addition to the articles, conference papers, and high-quality academic reports that he turned out during this period. Schramm also wrote several very influential texts, including *Mass Media and National Development.*[6] This book was an international best seller, studied by people throughout the world.

Schramm established a model of communication that attempts to explain the problems inherent in human communication. His models evolved in stages. They proceeded from a relatively simple individual form of communication to a complex model involving interaction between two parties.

In Schramm's first model, the *source* sends a message via an *encoder,* which is received by a *decoder* and transmitted to its designation. The *source* is the brain of the person starting the communications process. The *encoder* is the process by which ideas are converted to symbols for transmission to the other person. The *decoder* is the process by which the symbols are received and converted into ideas by the person receiving the information. The *signal* indicates that the symbols are produced and transmitted.

Schramm slowly modified this first model to include the concept that *only that information which is shared in the respective parties' fields of experience is actually communicated.* This is the only portion of the information that is communicated, because it is the only shared portion of the signal that is understood by both parties. Schramm's contribution to communications theory included the concept that each person has a field of experience that controls both the encoding and decoding of information and determines the meaning of that information.

Schramm's third model viewed communication as an interaction with both parties actively encoding, interpreting, decoding, transmitting, and receiving signals. He included the feedback of continuously shared information.

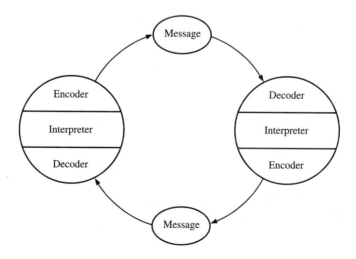

Schramm will be remembered as the father of communications and a remarkable scholar who formalized the study of this very important discipline. During the time period when Schramm was developing his theories, another leader in the field was perfecting a different perspective on communications. Harold Lasswell studied propaganda and created the *content analysis* method of communications research.

Lasswell's Model

Harold Lasswell (1902–1978) published over six million words during his lifetime. His doctoral dissertation, *Propaganda Techniques in the World War,* studied the effect of propaganda on people during World War I.[7] Lasswell defined propaganda as *the management of collective attitudes by the manipulation of significant symbols.* He did not necessarily consider propaganda bad or good; to him that determination depended on the sender's and receiver's points of view and whether the messages were truthful.[8]

Harold Lasswell is best known for one sentence: "Who says what in which channel to who with what effects?" In one of the early classics, Lasswell identifies five common variables in the communication process.[9] He states that one way to analyze the act of communication is to answer the following questions:

Who? When scholars analyze the *who* component they look at factors that initiate and guide the act of communication. This is called *control analysis.*

Says what? Scholars who examine this aspect of the communications process engage in *content analysis.*

In which channel? Scholars who look at the method or ways information travels engage in *data analysis.* They look at radio, press, film, and other channels of communication.

To whom? Scholars who investigate the persons reached by the media engage in *audience analysis.*

With what effect? Scholars who are concerned about the impact of the information on audiences study *effect analysis.*

Despite both being in Washington, D.C., during the war years of 1942 to 1945, Lasswell and Schramm did not meet until 1954, at Stanford. Like Schramm, Lasswell was a prolific scholar. He authored or coauthored over 300 articles and 52 books. Harold Lasswell pioneered content analysis methods and invented the qualitative and quantitative measurement of communications messages. He also introduced psychoanalytic theory into political science. Lasswell will be remembered as one of the giants in the study of communication.

GROUP VERSUS INDIVIDUAL COMMUNICATION

Up to this point we have been discussing the communication cycle without making any distinction between whether the process involves a one-on-one relationship or a situation among more than two people. Most of the information that has been presented applies to an interpersonal relationship. That is, a relationship between two persons. This might include a sergeant talking to a patrol officer or a lieutenant responding to a question from a captain. Many of the communication principles described in this chapter also apply to group communication. For example, feedback can occur at roll call when one patrol officer asks for clarification from the shift sergeant regarding the description of a rape suspect. For purposes of clarification, interpersonal communication may be defined as *the sharing of information between two persons.* Group communication involves interaction among three or more individuals in a face-to-face situation. The three people share a common need that is satisfied by the exchange of information.

The Size of the Group

The term *group* has been defined as *a number of persons gathered or classified together.*[10] The definition of group communication does not set limits on the ultimate size of the group. However, practical considerations inherent in the definition do define a maximum number of people that would be able to interact effectively. Individuals attending a professional sporting event may have a commonality of interest, but they may not have an opportunity to become involved in a face-to-face situation where they can exchange information that satisfies a common need. If we compare the Super Bowl, with an attendance of 100,000 people, to a group of 5 fans planning a tailgate party before the game, it is easy to see that the size of the group can be a factor in determining the ability of individuals to communicate with each other.

Numerous scholars have examined the dynamics of group communications.[11] Various research has determined that the range between 3 and 20 is a natural size for purposes of defining group interactions.[12] Once the size of the group exceeds 20 people, the ability of individual members to influence each other diminishes. The nature of the gathering takes on more of the characteristics of a mass meeting or conference in which one person may influence the group but the ability of individual members within the group to influence each other is limited. The size of the group has a direct bearing on the nature and type of communication involved. Therefore, we will limit our discussion of communication to groups that do not exceed 20 individuals.

Once the size of the group involved in the communication process has been determined, group interaction must be addressed.

Group Interaction

It is generally accepted by leading scholars, such as Fisher, that there are four phases in group interaction: (1) orientation, (2) conflict, (3) emergence, and (4) reinforcement.[13]

In the *orientation* phase, group members attempt to get to know each other and discover the problems that face the group. This may occur as strangers meet in a group for the first time, or it may happen with people who know each other and attend periodic meetings, such as roll call before the beginning of patrol shifts. In the latter situation, group members already know each other and the orientation is aimed at common problems facing the group. These problems could range from new shift hours to planning a social gathering after the shift.

The second phase, *conflict,* involves disagreement among the members of the group. This phase is characterized by an atmosphere of polarization and controversy. Using the previous two examples, patrol officers may be sharply divided concerning the benefits of the new shift hours or have strong feelings regarding the location of the social gathering.

During the *emergence* phase of group interaction, there is more emphasis on positive statements. This phase allows dissenting members to save face by moving toward the majority's position. Officers who oppose the new shift hours may begin to find other benefits that were not previously discussed. In a similar vein, the location for the party may be a third alternative that is acceptable to all members.

The final phase is *reinforcement.* This phase is the period when group members comment on the positive aspects of the group and its problem-solving ability.

The preceding discussion focused on the dynamics that normally occur in a problem-solving group; however, this interaction in one form or another will usually be present in most groups.[14] A police officer may determine what phase a group is in by listening to the types of comments being made by members of the group, then use that information to express personal views in the most effective manner. Group interaction is an important aspect of any organization. Law enforcement officers need to understand these group dynamics in order to carry out their duties effectively.

Communication Patterns

Anyone who has observed a group of people discussing a topic has observed that not everyone in the group spends the same amount of time talking. Information flows according to status or power. Generally, persons with high status or actual or perceived power send and receive more messages than other members of the group.[15] These persons serve as the hub for group communications. They will receive and send more messages than any other member of the group.

Once a group has been established, certain communication dynamics begin to emerge. A *communications network* is the pattern of information that flows among members of a group. After a group has been in existence and functioning for a period of time, certain members will repeatedly talk with other members. This forms a network over which information flows within the group.

Another communication dynamic that takes place in group communication concerns the *centrality of communication. Centrality* is the degree of centralization of the message flow and decision making. In a more centralized group's communication pattern, information is funneled to one or two persons with high status or power, who then transmit the same message to other members of the group.

The classic studies of Leavitt and Bavelas established that more decentralized communication networks are faster in solving complex problems, and centralized networks are more efficient in dealing with less complex issues.[16] However, efficiency in problem solving should not be the only factor considered by the officer. Studies indicate that members of decentralized communication networks experience a greater degree of satisfaction with their participation in the group.[17]

Communication patterns within a group are an important part of the communication process. An intelligent police officer will take the time to understand these patterns and ensure that they are used to the advantage of the department.

The group and individual communication cycle is a dynamic and changing environment. While it is difficult to communicate on an individual basis, a law enforcement officer should not despair at having to communicate with a group. Careful study and persistence will allow one to communicate effectively and thus become a leader within the department.

SUMMARY

Communication plays an important role in our personal and professional life. Up to 70 percent of our work time is spent communicating with others. Communication is a process involving several steps, between two or more persons, for the primary purpose of exchanging information. This process requires sending an idea, receipt of that idea by the other party, an understanding of the idea, and feedback to the sender of the message.

The Johari window is a communication model that allows police officers to examine their ability to communicate with subordinates and superiors effectively. The window is divided into four panes that represent basic areas of knowledge. The Johari window establishes four basic types of communication patterns: Type A has very little feedback or exposure, Type B does not transmit information to subordinates, Type C is characterized by constantly expressing opinions and refusing to accept feedback from others, and Type D emphasizes open lines of communication with feedback from all parties. Schramm and Lasswell are considered to be early pioneers in the field of communications. They also established models of communication. These models further explain this complex interchange of information.

While most of the principles of the communication process apply to both groups and individuals, certain interpersonal dynamics occur in a group setting.

The police officer should understand these interactions so as to be able to communicate in any situation.

REVIEW QUESTIONS

1. Describe the concept behind the Johari window. What is the purpose of this concept?
2. How can use of the Johari window make you a better communicator?
3. Since police officers work in a quasi-military organization whose members follow orders, why should they understand the concepts involved in group communication?

BETTER WRITING DRILLS

In the Better Writing Drills in this chapter, we examine the use of the *first person,* use of the *active voice,* and correct use of *pronouns.*

First Person

Use of the first person means referring to yourself as *I* rather than *this officer.* In the past, many police officers were taught to use the third person rather than the first person. The first person is recommended because it is clearer and more direct. For example:

> *This officer* arrested the suspect.
> *I* arrested the suspect.

> *This officer* saw the victim sitting in the street.
> *I* saw the victim sitting in the street.

Use of the Active Voice

Sentences may be written in either the active or passive voice. Clear writing generally requires the use of active sentences. To determine if active or passive words are used, apply the following test:

Locate the subject and verb of a sentence. Remember, the subject tells *who* and the verb tells *what was done.* If the subject performed the action, then the sentence is *active.* If the subject did not perform the action, then the sentence is *passive.* What was done? Did the subject of the sentence do it? If so, the sentence is an active sentence.

> *Active:* The accused fired the gun.
> *Passive:* The gun was fired by the accused.
> *Active:* The accused did not fire the gun.

Passive: The gun was not fired by the accused.

Active: The suspect drove the car.

Passive: The car was driven by the suspect.

The use of the passive sentence may be appropriate if the doer of the action is unknown:

Someone fired the gun three times.

Better: The gun was fired three times.

(Individual who fired the gun was unknown.)

The passive sentence may also be appropriate if you wish to call attention to the receiver of the action rather than the doer.

The victim was hit by the accused.

The passive sentence is also used to prevent embarrassment of the doer.

The training was canceled because Sergeant Williams failed to order the proper equipment.

Better: The training was canceled because the proper equipment was not ordered.

Correct Use of Pronouns

A *pronoun* is a word used in place of a noun.

Noun	Pronoun
Joe	he
Joe and Jill	they
Jill	she
the gun	it

Pronouns should refer to only one person or object. The most common mistake when using pronouns is the unclear pronoun reference. For example, "When I nod my head, hit it." This is a classic example of unclear pronoun reference. In case of doubt, do not use the pronoun. For example, "When I nod my head, hit the nail."

Poor pronoun reference can be observed in the following sentences:

The suspect told the police officer he had made a mistake.

The officer read the suspect the *Miranda* warnings which he understood.

The suspect was seen by the apartment manager while he was in the elevator.

Whom does *he* refer to?

PRACTICAL APPLICATIONS

1. Select five students. Have one of the students write out a five-sentence state-
    ment. That student should then orally repeat the statement to the next student.
    The student who receives the message should repeat it to another student and so
    on until the oral message ends up back at the first student. Have the first student
    repeat the oral message and read the original written message.

2. Listen to another person and see if you can repeat everything that person says to
    you during a three-minute conversation.

3. Are there any physical barriers to effective listening in your classroom? What
    are they? Can you do anything to improve the situation?

4. Identify each statement that is written in the third person and change it to the
    first person:

    a. This officer pulled his gun and pointed it at the suspect.

    b. This arresting officer pulled his gun and pointed it at the suspect.

    c. This investigating officer questioned each victim.

    d. This traffic officer stopped the driver of the stolen vehicle.

5. Which of the following sentences are written in the active voice? For those writ-
    ten in the passive voice, rewrite them to change them to the active voice.

    a. The car was stolen by the accused.

    b. The house was broken into by Joe.

    c. The case was tried by the new deputy attorney.

    d. The police officer read the suspect his rights.

    e. A confession was given by the accused.

6. Improve the following sentences by correcting any faulty pronoun references:

    a. Angered by the language, Jerry told Jim that he would have to leave.

    b. After the robber took the gun from the purse, he threw it into the river.

    c. Joe told Jim that he would soon be a police officer.

    d. The chief told the police officer that he was in good health.

    e. If the preface of a book bores me, I do not read it.

7. In each of the rows below, circle the correctly spelled word:

    | handerchief | handkerchief | handkrchief | handkercheif |
    | hereditary | hearditary | herditarty | harditary |
    | narcoitic | narocotic | narcotic | narccotic |
    | loitering | liotering | loiterring | liotering |
    | maintennance | maintenance | maintanence | maintenonce |

objecteively	objecteviley	ojectivily	objectively
obstrcuted	obstructted	obstrucked	obstructed
qualification	qualifcation	qualificattion	quailification
sobatage	sobotage	sabatage	sabotage
subponena	subpoena	subpeona	subpeono

8. Rewrite the following sentences as needed:

   a. The car was driven by the offender from the robbery.

   _____

   b. The subjects gun was fired at the victim by the offender.

   _____

   c. This officer arrived at the scene and arrested the victim's assaulter.

   _____

   d. The wanted person was observed by a citizen while he was in a school.

   _____

   e. Who and why aren't you going?

   _____

9. Define and explain the following words or terms:

   a. encoder

   _____

   b. signal

   _____

   c. Johari window

   _____

   d. Schramm's model

   _____

   e. Lasswell's model

   _____

10. The following paragraph was taken from an actual police report. Make it a better paragraph.

    It should be noted that while both offenders were facing each other this officer observed the condition of both faces. Subject Wolson's face had a small cut below the right eye which appeared as if subject Wolson had been hit by subject Hamm. Subject Hamm had a back eye that could have been caused by subject Wolson. This officer asked each subject what had happened and each subject claimed that the other subject had hit him. At this point, this officer suspected that the two subjects had been fitghtin amoung themselves.

_____

_____

_____

_____

_____

WORDS TO KNOW

accumulate	implement
accurate	linoleum
bulletin	native
campaign	occurrence
confidentiality	practice
digit	proceed
domestic	receive
enough	replied
feminine	revolver
grievance	signature

ENDNOTES

1. The following material is adapted from Joseph Luft, *Group Processes: An Introduction to Group Dynamics* (Palo Alto, Calif.: Mayfield, 1970) and Joseph Luft, *Of Human Interaction* (Palo Alto, Calif.: National Press Books, 1969).

2. J. Hall, "Interpersonal Style and the Communication Dilemma: Management Implications of the Johari Awareness Model," *Human Relations* 27, no. 4 (Apr. 1974): 381.

3. Wilbur Schramm, "How Communications Works," in Wilbur Schramm, ed., *The Process and Effects of Mass Communications* (Urbana, Ill.: University of Illinois Press, 1955).

4. Everett M. Rogers, *A History of Communication Study* (New York: Free Press, 1994).

5. Emile McAnany, "Wilbur Schramm, 1907–1987: Roots of the Past, Seeds of the Present," *Journal of Communication* 38, no. 4 (1988): 109–122.

6. Wilbur Schramm, *Mass Media and National Development* (Stanford, Calif.: Stanford University Press, 1964).

7. Harold Lasswell, *Propaganda Techniques in the World War* (New York: Knopf, 1927; New York: Peter Smith, 1938; Cambridge, Mass.: The MIT Press, 1971).

8. Everett M. Rogers, *A History of Communication Study* (New York: Free Press, 1994).

9. Harold Lasswell, "The Structure and Function of Communication in Society," in L. Bryson, ed., *The New Communication of Ideas* (New York: Harper & Brothers, 1948).

10. *Webster's New World Dictionary* (New York: Warner Books, 1990), 262.

11. See Michael Burgoon, Judee K. Heston, and James McCroskey, *Small Group Communication: A Functional Approach* (New York: Holt, Rinehart & Winston, 1974), 2–3.

12. See Robert Ardrey, *The Social Contract* (New York: Atheneum, 1970), 368, where the author theorizes that the range for a natural group is 11 or 12; and Marvin E. Shaw, *Group Dynamics* (New York: McGraw-Hill, 1971), which places the maximum number of persons at 20.

13. B. Aubrey Fisher, "Decision Emergence: Phase in Group Decision-Making," *Speech Monographs* 37 (1970): 53–66.

14. Mark W. Field, "The Abilene Paradox," *Law and Order* (Mar. 1995): 89.

15. Barry E. Collins and Harold Guetzkow, *A Social Psychology of Group Processes for Decision-Making* (New York: John Wiley, 1964), 170–77.

16. See H. J. Leavitt, "Some Effects of Certain Communication Patterns on Group Performance," *Journal of Abnormal and Social Psychology* 465(1951): 38–50; and Alex Bavelas, "Communication Patterns in Task-Oriented Groups," *Journal of Acoustical Society* 22 (1950): 725–30.

17. Leavitt, "Some Effects of Certain Communication Patterns on Group Performance," 38–50.

4

Improving Communication

KEY TERMS

Feedback—Process that allows persons transmitting information to correct and adjust messages to adapt to the receiver.

Physical barriers—Those aspects of our environment that make communication more difficult.

Semantics—The study of the development and meaning of words.

Semantic problems—The inability to agree on the meaning of certain terms, with a resulting loss in the ability to communicate clearly.

In this chapter, we look at how to improve communication. First, the barriers to communication and the various types of feedback are discussed. Understanding both the barriers to communication and the concept of feedback are critical to the communication process.

BARRIERS TO COMMUNICATION

In earlier chapters, we examined how information flows from one person to another. On the surface, sending and receiving information appears to be an easy task, one that anybody could successfully accomplish. However, as we all know and have undoubtedly experienced, numerous pitfalls await those who try to express themselves clearly on a personal level. These pitfalls or barriers become more troublesome when we attempt to communicate in a professional or working environment.[1] This section examines the various barriers to effective communication in a law enforcement setting. Barriers to communication often arise when one party is concerned about personal or professional status.[2] The four basic categories or types of obstacles to effective communication are: (1) emotional, (2) physical, (3) semantic, and (4) ineffective listening. Each of these barriers can cause either the sender or the receiver to fail to communicate effectively.

Emotional Barriers

Emotional barriers may be present in either the sender or receiver. We base our encoding or transmitting of information on our own experiences and expectations. An officer who expects to be rejected or laughed at for a suggestion or comment will not send that message. The need to preserve our self-esteem is universal. Individuals with low self-esteem use certain patterns when attempting to communicate.[3] Some may use *tag questions* at the end of a sentence. For example, a tag question would be phrased, "This is an interesting case, *isn't it?*" Others with low self-esteem use qualifiers or disclaimers in everyday speech. Qualifying phrases include "sort of" or "perhaps"; disclaimers include such phrases as "I really don't think this is a good idea." When we hedge or qualify language, it becomes less clear and our true intent is often hidden. An officer who suffers from low self-esteem may not be forthcoming in opinions regarding the cause of an accident or who committed a crime. Generally, low self-esteem translates into the inability to make an assertive statement. Other emotional barriers that cause communications to break down range from simple depression to complex psychological problems.

In an effort to address emotional problems within law enforcement departments, some agencies have developed peer support systems.[4] These programs are designed to implement small interventions before the situation develops into an emotional crisis for an officer. Peer support involves officers working with each other to solve problems. Many departments also use peer support in conjunction with other professional help when an officer has been involved in a shooting or other critical incident.

Physical Barriers

Physical barriers are those aspects of our environment that make communication more difficult. These barriers include a rigid chain of command that requires the officer to report to a supervisor instead of informing a peer of information obtained regarding a crime. Equipment malfunctions, such as a faulty radio or computer, are another source of physical barriers to effective communication. Even such a simple thing as the distance between officers conducting a search of a wooded area is a type of physical barrier. Any obstruction that slows or impedes the free flow of information is a physical barrier to communication.

Semantic Barriers

Semantics is the third form of communication barrier. Strictly speaking, semantics is the study of the development and meaning of words. However, semantic problems can be defined as *the inability to agree on the meaning of certain terms with a resulting loss in the ability to communicate clearly.*[5] When Officer Jones states, "He is a real juvenile delinquent," other officers may come to several different conclusions regarding what Officer Jones means. One officer may interpret the statement as meaning that the suspect is a minor with repeated convictions in the juvenile justice system. Another officer may believe Officer Jones is opining that the suspect, while under the age of 18, is simply acting out and is not a hard-core criminal. A third officer may mistake the focus of the comment and believe that Officer Jones is discussing a fellow officer who acts immaturely!

Ineffective Listening

The final barrier to effective communication is the inability to hear or receive what the other party is transmitting.[6] As a group, people—including police officers and administrators—are poor listeners. There are numerous reasons for this deficiency. In addition, there are other factors that cause a person to be inattentive in any given situation. First, the subject under discussion may be boring or irrelevant to the listener's interests. Second, the topic of the conversation may be too complex or too simple for the listener. Finally, the listener may be preoccupied with personal problems.

The general cause of ineffective listening is *habit,* which can be traced back to the individual's earliest development. The pattern of being a talker rather than a listener is learned during childhood. As children, when we cry or tell our parents we are hurt, we receive attention. This pattern continues during the early school years, when students are encouraged to assert themselves. Schools tend to produce good talkers but poor listeners because the emphasis is on self-assertion. Talking is a form of potential power, a way to control others, to change their ideas, to shape their reality. We all use language in this manner, whether we are a presidential candidate trying to gain popular support, a student attempting to get a grade change, or a six-year-old child trying to obtain a parental favor.

Talking is a basic emotional need. To be heard is to be recognized by others. Through words, people can relieve tension or punish others for their acts.

There are four general variables relating to listening. First, the listener has to have the ability to absorb what is heard based on experience, education, and verbal proficiency. Second, the ability of the speaker to transmit the message effectively affects the listener's attention span. Third, the message being transmitted must be of interest to the listener. The fourth factor is that the environment in which communication takes place affects the listener's ability to receive the information.

All of us will probably recognize from experience that certain factors cause us to tune out certain messages. An effective listener guards against the following barriers:

- *Uninteresting topic*—The officer may not be interested in what the speaker is saying. The officer may already be aware of the problem or issue that is being discussed.
- *Critique of the speaker*—There may be a bias against the speaker because of the speaker's manner of expression.

- *Emotional involvement*—In some situations the officer may be excited, and the stress will interfere with the communication process.
- *Failure to adjust to distractions*—Officers must listen to different people within a short period of time. A police officer may interview a victim, interrogate a suspect, and receive instructions from the sergeant all within an hour. The administrator may receive information from a subordinate, sit in a meeting with the chief, and attend a community relations luncheon within that same time period. The effective listener must be able to adjust to new situations quickly and screen out distractions so as to receive the information that is transmitted.
- *Emotionally laden words*—Regardless of context, certain words may be offensive. The officer's reaction to these words may interfere with the ability to listen critically, free from bias.

Effective listening requires an environment and training that is conducive to concentration. An officer must constantly attempt to improve listening skills.

Since listening is the opposite of speaking, these processes overlap to form the more general activity of communication. Certain steps in the listening process are important to police officers.

First, the officer should try to avoid developing a preconceived notion of the speaker or the message. The officer must scrutinize the speaker's motives, viewpoint, and accuracy, but should not make any conclusions until after listening attentively to the speaker. The officer should not try to anticipate what the speaker will say, because this will influence the manner in which the officer interprets the speaker's message. In effect, people will hear what they expect and want to hear if they anticipate the message.

Effective Listening Exercise 1

If the officer arrives at the scene of a crime and is approached by a tall male with a beard, hair in a pony tail, wearing dirty clothes, what type of preconceived notions may the officer have?

1. A street bum, who didn't see anything.
2. A long-haired hippie, probably on dope.
3. An undercover detective, who can assist in the investigation.

Second, the officer may work in a city or state where many language systems are used. Ethnic groups abound in many jurisdictions and each uses the English language differently. Officers must be certain that they and the speakers are indeed speaking and interpreting the same language.

Effective Listening Exercise 2

Upon arriving at the scene of a crime, the officer is approached by a person speaking a foreign language that the officer cannot understand. What should the officer do?

Finally, as a listener the officer must make an effort to retain the message for later use. At a minimum, the officer must be able to retain the message until the substance of it is recorded in a written report.

Effective Listening Exercise 3

Many times officers will be in situations that prevent them from writing down information immediately. Suggest some ways officers can remember a description of a suspect until they can write it down.

The value of effective listening in police work is twofold: it enhances the investigative function and improves relations with individuals, both within the department and with members of the public who come into contact with police officers. Put simply, poor listening increases the difficulty of functioning in a law enforcement environment.

Barriers to effective communication prevent transmitting information clearly and rapidly. At the same time, they may prevent the other party from receiving the intended message. One method to ensure that the intended message has been received is through the use of feedback. The next section examines this important aspect of communication.

FEEDBACK

Sending and receiving a message does not end the communication cycle. It is incumbent on any law enforcement officer to ensure that the information transmitted is understood by the receiving party. This is where *feedback* enters the picture. Without feedback, officers talk or transmit into a black hole that absorbs all the information and does not give any indication that it was received, was understood, or will be acted on. Communicating without feedback is very similar to ordering a product and not including a return address. You realize something is wrong only after the fact, when the product fails to arrive.

Types of Feedback

Norbert Wiener, a cybernetics scholar, defined feedback as "the property of being able to adjust future conduct by past performance. Feedback may be as simple as that of the common reflex or it may be a higher order feedback, in which past experience is used not only to regulate specific movements, but also whole polices of behavior."[7] While this definition may seem at first glance to be very technical, it can be reworded more simply to define feedback as "that process that allows persons transmitting information to correct and adjust messages to adapt to the receiver." Utilizing this definition, it becomes clear that feedback is not a single act, but rather a series of acts that allows the sender to understand that the other person has received the information. Just as feedback is not a single act, so should it be clear that there is more than one type of feedback.

Direct Feedback In the most simple of feedback messages, the receiver consciously and intentionally constructs feedback that is sent directly back to the transmitter of the message. "Sergeant, I don't understand what you want me to do" is an example of direct feedback that a patrol officer might use to indicate that the sergeant's message is unclear. This type of feedback is also known as *purposive* feedback.[8]

Indirect Feedback This is a more subtle form of feedback. As its name implies, indirect feedback is not information that is intentionally sent to the transmitter. It may take many forms; for example, nonverbal actions by the receiver may indicate the message is not interesting. The lack of eye contact, the shifting of the body, or a yawn may indicate that the message is not one the receiver has any interest in understanding or acting on. This type of feedback is known as *nonpurposive*.[9]

Positive Feedback This feedback indicates that the receiver is happy or pleased with the message received. This feedback may be nonverbal—a smile or nod—or verbal: "Thanks for your advice on this project, Lieutenant." This type of feedback indicates that the person has not only received the message, but approves of the content.

Negative Feedback This is the other side of positive feedback. It informs the transmitter that the receiver does not agree with the content of the message. Both positive and negative feedback are important in the communication process. Positive feedback encourages the transmitter to continue to send messages, and negative feedback informs the transmitter that certain information does not please the receiver.

Immediate Feedback This feedback usually occurs in a face-to-face meeting. It may be nonverbal or verbal, but is of great value in immediately understanding whether the message has been clearly understood. However, there are occasions when immediate feedback may not be wise or productive even in a face-to-face personal setting. If the situation is emotional or tense, immediate feedback may not be understood or acted on. In some of these situations, delayed feedback may be the appropriate form of interaction.

Delayed Feedback Delayed feedback may occur when departmental memorandums are circulated. In these situations, officers may respond orally or in writing, indicating their feelings about a directive or memorandum. One of the problems with utilizing delayed feedback is that it does not inform the sender that the message was received and understood immediately. The sender must wait to confirm the validity of the information until the feedback is received.

The preceding discussion indicates there are various forms of feedback. However, these forms may merge to allow feedback in a combination of ways. For example, you might have direct, negative, or delayed feedback on a message or any combination thereof. The various types of feedback form a basis for understanding in the communication process. The next section examines how feedback is received by the sender.

Receiving Feedback

Receiving feedback involves the process of effective listening. However, receiving feedback is more than simply being an effective listener. To initiate the process of receiving feedback, the officer must make an open attempt to encourage such action. Citizens hesitate to attempt to clarify a message from a law enforcement officer. There are a number of reasons for this hesitancy: fear of rejection, anger on the part of the officer, failure of the officer to act on the feedback, and clear indications from the officer that no feedback is wanted are a few of the more common factors. All of these reasons can be traced to the actions or perceptions of the law enforcement officer.

The police officer must take the first step in the process. Officers should ensure that everyone understands that they are open to honest comments regarding any information they transmit. Effective leaders not only state that they believe in these principles; more important, their actions support this belief. Cops on the street are great judges of character, and they can tell a phony—whether it is a con artist bilking senior citizens out of their life savings or a superior officer who mouths "communication principles" and then ignores them.

A Police Department Receives Feedback from the Community

Citizens of Clearwater, Florida, are considered "customers" of the police department. And, as any well-run organization knows, what your customers think of your business is important. With this in mind, the police department developed a "customer satisfaction" survey to better serve the needs of the citizenry.

Traditional survey methods such as phone calls, letters, and so forth, are inadequate to determine a department's effectiveness. Most people call or write only if they are very happy or extremely unhappy with the way the department responds to their specific complaint. The middle ground and overall judgment are lost.

The Clearwater Police Department and the Clearwater City Managers' Office developed an 11-page survey with 32 questions designed to obtain feedback in two main areas: (1) the feelings and concerns of the respondents about their neighborhoods, and (2) the respondents' feelings about the performance of the police department and its employees.

Police management uses the survey to get feedback on public concerns and opinions of the department in general. It also enables the public to grade the department on the way it looks and the efficiency of its operations. The survey has opened avenues of communication that have traditionally been closed and is certainly an asset to the department.

Source: Adapted from Douglas L. Griffith, "Citizen Feedback Line," *Law and Order* (Dec. 1993): 37.

The decision to encourage feedback involves taking a risk. It is probable that a police officer will at some time in his or her career receive information that is not pleasing or is threatening to the ego. An effective listener must be a risk taker. This doesn't mean attempting to stop an armed robbery single-handed; it means accepting the principle that gains in efficiency in operating the division can occur only if someone is open and willing to change.

Receiving feedback is not an easy process. It takes constant attention and an honest desire to improve the ability to communicate. However, the rewards are immeasurable. The individual who accepts feedback becomes a more effective officer.

Giving Feedback

The receipt of feedback is only a portion of the feedback process. It is equally important that a police officer understand how to give feedback. Any law enforcement officer must be a problem solver. This requires not only being receptive to receiving feedback but being able to give feedback effectively.

Giving feedback requires sensitivity to the person who is to receive the information. Some general guidelines any manager should use when giving feedback follow:

- *The person who is receiving the feedback must trust the officer.* Giving feedback must not be part of any power game or attempt to play one party against another. The party receiving the feedback must be able to accept the information at face value to act on it. This involves the establishment of a trusting relationship or, at the very least, the acknowledgment that the information being transmitted is for the purposes stated and that there is no hidden agenda on the part of the officer.
- *Feedback should be timely.* It is not effective to tell a citizen that you didn't understand his or her report two weeks after it was submitted. Feedback must

be given and received by the other party in sufficient time to react to the information.

- *Feedback must be given in an understanding, sensitive manner.* If an officer humiliates private citizens by telling them that they can't express themselves and are therefore stupid, other citizens will not readily accept comments from that officer in the future. On the other hand, if the officer points out the positive aspects of citizens' statements or reports, and indicates that while they are good there can still be some improvement, the citizens will not be as hesitant to ask for or receive feedback from the officer in the future.

- *Feedback must be factual.* The police officer must ensure that there is a factual orientation to comments to citizens. Simply saying, "I don't understand your statement" does not give the citizen receiving the feedback any details or facts on which to act. However, saying "Your statement indicates the attack occurred at night—I need to know what time during the evening the attack occurred," will ensure that the citizen understands the area that needs to be improved.

- *The process of giving feedback should be consistent.* The law enforcement officer must embark on a process of timely, accurate, and sensitive feedback on a daily basis with subordinates, superiors, and citizens. Once this pattern is established, it should become an accepted part of the officer's style.

Giving feedback is an essential part of becoming and remaining an effective police officer. It improves the relationships between subordinates, superiors, and citizens. Feedback allows increased cooperation among all the parties involved in the process.

Using Feedback

Giving and receiving feedback is useless unless the police officer is willing to use it and is capable of doing so. The term *using feedback* is used to describe how the superior responds to feedback or acts when giving feedback. As stated previously, feedback is part of the communication process and it may involve simply clarifying transmitted information. However, feedback can also result in changed relationships between the law enforcement manager and superiors as well as subordinates. This change in relationship can result from either a modified perception on the part of others regarding the manager or a change in the manager's actions as a result of the feedback process.

The preceding sections have already examined the techniques involved in clarifying information that is sent from one party to another. This section briefly reviews how officers may change their behavior when sending or receiving feedback. Behavior modification is one of the hardest things any of us can undertake; however, the reward for the police officer will be a more effective law enforcement agency.

Feedback should never be given when an officer is angry. This poses a dilemma since feedback should be timely. If the officer waits to cool off, the window of opportunity for effective feedback may have passed. The police officer must therefore learn to integrate emotions and feelings with intellect and reason. It is perfectly normal to respond with anger in some situations. The critical issue is to accept the emotion and review the cause of it. The officer should work toward an expanded vocabulary so as to become more expressive of feelings without resorting to raising the voice.

When receiving feedback, managers should paraphrase the information in their own words. This allows officers to state how they interpret the other person's ideas and feelings. Police officers should practice *parasupporting*. This is a technique in which an officer not only paraphrases the other's comments but also carries those ideas further by providing examples or other data that the officer believes will help to illustrate and clarify those ideas.[10]

Using feedback effectively is critical to improving relations within a law enforcement department. Feedback is the glue that holds the communications cycle together. The feedback process is not one we fall into naturally; however, with practice it will enhance the police officers' interpersonal relationships and allow them to become more effective officers.

SUMMARY

There are several barriers to communication. These range from emotional feelings to physical obstacles that prevent the free flow of information. While not a barrier per se, the failure to listen can disrupt the flow of data from one party to another. Effective listening is a technique that anyone can learn.

Feedback is the process that allows persons transmitting messages to adapt to the receiver. There are various forms of feedback, all of which may be combined or merged to present data to the person transmitting the message. Receiving and giving feedback are processes that enhance the ability of police officers to effectively communicate with others.

REVIEW QUESTIONS

1. Of the barriers to communication discussed in this chapter, which one is the easiest to overcome? Justify your answer.
2. What is the most common type of feedback?
3. What is the importance of feedback?
4. How are listening and speaking interconnected?
5. What can we do to improve our listening skills?

BETTER WRITING DRILLS

In this chapter, the Better Writing Drills discuss *misplaced modifiers, squinting modifiers, dangling modifiers,* and *parallelism.*

Misplaced Modifiers

As noted earlier, clear writing requires that modifiers not be separated from the words they modify. Accordingly, modifiers should be placed as close as possible to the words they modify. This is especially true of words such as *almost, just, merely,* and *only.*

Examples

Wrong: The accused bought a gun from a man in Texas with a broken firing pin.

Better: The accused bought a gun with a broken firing pin from a man in Texas.

Wrong: The accused only shot one victim.

Better: The accused shot only one victim.

Wrong: The briefcase was found in the hall doorway partly opened.

Better: The partly opened briefcase was found in the hall doorway.

Squinting Modifiers

Squinting modifiers are those modifiers that seem to modify both the word they follow and the word they precede. Accordingly, the sentence has two possible meanings. Modifiers should clearly modify only one word or phrase.

Examples

Wrong: The accused decided at that instant to fire his gun.

Better: At that instant, the accused decided to fire his gun.

Wrong: The accused had planned with his friend to rob the bank.

Better: The accused and his friend had planned to rob the bank.

Dangling Modifiers

One morning I shot an elephant in my pajamas. How he got in my pajamas I'll never know.

—Groucho Marx

Local Woman Hospitalized by Accident

—Headline in a Colorado newspaper

A dangling modifier is a word or group of words that do not refer clearly or logically to any other word in the sentence. Place modifiers in a position so that they clearly and directly refer to a word or phrase in the sentence.

Examples

Wrong: Before arresting him, the suspect was informed of his rights.

Better: The suspect was informed of his rights before he was arrested.

Wrong: To hide the evidence of the crime, the body was burned.

Better: He burned the body to hide the evidence of the crime.

Wrong: Completely exhausted, I saw the man collapse to the floor.

Better: I saw the completely exhausted man collapse to the floor.

Parallelism

Parallelism results when two or more grammatically equivalent sentence elements are joined. Accordingly, faulty parallelism results when dissimilar elements are joined. Clear writing uses parallelism.

Examples

Wrong: The officer drew a deep breath and his eyes closed. (*Active/Passive*)

Better: The officer drew a deep breath and closed his eyes. (*Active/Active*)

Wrong: The overproduction of goods and having easy money policies both contributed to the Depression. (Note that the verb phrase *having easy money* is not parallel to the noun phrase *the overproduction of goods.*)

Better: The overproduction of goods and easy money policies contributed to the Depression.

PRACTICAL APPLICATIONS

1. Rewrite the following sentences to eliminate misplaced, squinting, or dangling modifiers:
   a. Without asking to be repaid, the officer almost gave us all the money we needed.
   b. The door that he opened quickly closed.
   c. The rains that the crops had needed badly damaged the roads.
   d. Situated in San Francisco, tourists will enjoy Fisherman's Wharf.
   e. When in Houston, the heat and humidity may be a discomfort to visitors.
   f. To see Washington at its best, a walking tour is recommended.

2. Rewrite the following sentences to correct errors, if any, in parallelism:
   a. The police officer should be neat and cleaner.
   b. Running is better exercise than to walk.
   c. Acting wisely is more difficult than to think wise.
   d. The burglar was obviously inexperienced and not well educated.
   e. The police want respect and to be liked.

3. In each of the rows below, circle the correctly spelled word:

strangaluton	strungulation	strangulation	strangulaton
seducetion	seduction	secdiction	sudection
sowage	sowege	sewoge	sewage
sargeant	sargaent	sergeant	sargeant
secretery	secretary	secratery	secretory
prohebited	prohibeted	prohibited	prehibited
prosepective	prospective	prospecteve	prosspective
promisory	promissery	promisery	promissory
proistitution	proistitution	prostitution	prostutition
pursuade	persuade	purseade	pursuede

4. Rewrite the following sentences as needed:
   a. He ate fast because she had already ate.

   _____

   b. The food smelled awfully.

   _____

   c. His mood changed sudden.

   _____

   d. The offender was heavy armed.

   _____

   e. He admitted that he was mistake.

   _____

5. Define and explain the following words or terms:
   a. feedback

   _____

   b. semantics

   _____

   c. emotional barriers to communication

   _____

   d. physical barriers to communication

   _____

   e. parallelism

   _____

6. The following paragraph was taken from an actual police report. Make it a better paragraph.

> This officer caused the subjects to be transported to the city police department where he was placed in a detention cell. The subjects were arrested and booked under the suspision of distrubing the peace. No further action was taken by this officer except writing this report.

_____

_____

_____

_____

_____

WORDS TO KNOW

electronic	jewelry
eligible	language
evaluate	minimum
exaggerate	occupant
experience	personal
feedback	prejudice
flexible	relieve
furniture	separate
guarantee	stopped
identification	written

ENDNOTES

1. See Carl R. Rogers and F. J. Roethlisberger's classic article, "Barriers and Gateways to Communication," *Harvard Business Review* (Nov.–Dec. 1991): 105–111, for an excellent discussion of barriers to communication.

2. Mervin Kohn, *Dynamic Managing* (Menlo Park, Calif.: Cummings, 1977).

3. Mervin D. Lynch, "Stylistic Analysis," in Philip Emmert and William D. Brooks, eds., *Method of Research in Communications* (New York: Houghton Miffin, 1970), 315–342.

4. James Janik, "Who Needs Peer Support?" *The Police Chief* (Jan. 1995): 38.

5. Barbara Marquand, "How Are We Doing?" *Law and Order* (Dec. 1994): 41.

6. This section is adapted from "Effective Listening," International Association of Chiefs of Police Training Key Series, no. 290 (Alexandria, Va.).

7. Norbert Wiener, *Cybernetics* (New York: John Wiley, 1948), 33.

8. John Keltner, *Interpersonal Communications: Elements and Structures* (Belmont, Calif.: Wadsworth, 1970), 92.

9. Ibid., 92.

10. John Stewart and Gary D'Angelo, "Responsive Listening," in Jean M. Civilly, ed., *Messages: A Reader in Human Communication* (New York: Random House, 1977), 191, 192.

5

Special Communications Issues

LEARNING OBJECTIVES

After reading this chapter, you should understand the following concepts:
• Why it is desirable to understand other cultures.
• How some law enforcement agencies are learning Spanish.
• How to communicate with a person who has a hearing impairment.

KEY TERMS

Signing—Movement of hands, body, and face to communicate.

Ameslan—American Sign Language, the sign language used by persons who have hearing impairments.

Previous chapters examined the process of communication and its impact on criminal justice personnel. The principles described in those chapters apply to the operations of any police department as well as many other government entities and private businesses. This chapter reviews communications issues that are especially important to law enforcement departments. The focus of this chapter is on those communication skills needed by the officer on the street, whether that person is a patrol officer working traffic or a homicide investigator. By the very nature of its mission, a law enforcement agency has unique issues that are not found in any other organization. No other bureaucracy in the free world holds the power of life and death over other human beings. The duties and requirements of police officers are distinct from those of any other job. With these different job requirements comes the need for special communication skills in a variety of situations.

Communicating with other cultures or encountering a foreign language during a routine patrol is becoming more and more common. Our cities, counties, and states are becoming more populated and the number of different cultures within any given area is increasing. In many of our major metropolitan cities, there are areas completely occupied by specific groups of people from different cultures. An officer must be prepared to communicate effectively in this environment.[1] As persons with hearing impairments continue to enter the mainstream of life, they need the assistance of law enforcement personnel. The person with a hearing impairment is one of the most misunderstood individuals in modern society.

COMMUNICATION WITH OTHER CULTURES

This is an area in law enforcement that is still evolving. The United States is a melting pot for other races and cultures. With the increase of Southeast Asian refugees and the increasing Hispanic population, the problem of communicating with persons who do not speak English as a primary language is critical within the law enforcement community.[2]

Survival Spanish[3]

Hispanics constitute the fastest growing minority group in the United States. Population experts predict that this group will outnumber African-Americans by the end of the first quarter of the 21st century.

Development of "Survival Spanish for Police Officers" began in mid-1986 at Sam Houston State University, in a cooperative effort between the police academy and a faculty member of the university's Spanish department. The cross-cultural training grew from a minor part of the language component when it became apparent that cultural barriers were just as important as the language barrier and had to be addressed in more detail.

Spanish Language Component (8 hours)

Curriculum: Instruction begins with a crash course in Spanish pronunciation that emphasizes eliminating problems with the most troublesome sounds for Anglos learning Spanish. To help with pronunciation, a list of the 50 most common Spanish names is used for practice. The gain is twofold: not only are officers given an opportunity to work with single-word units (names), but they also quickly perfect the pronunciation of the very names they will encounter on the street. The class then learns to read the *Miranda* warning in Spanish, thus moving to entire sentence units. This increases the officers' confidence and level of comfort with unfamiliar Spanish sounds.

The core of the day consists of four one-hour classes that include a total of 39 "survival" commands, questions, warnings, and exchanges. Some of the items included are "Sit down," "Shut up," "I'm a police officer," "Stop," "Get out of the car," and "Put the weapon down." The Spanish equivalents are taught as purely rote items to be mastered quickly through a variety of language techniques. The last session of the day is devoted to simulations and role playing in which officers act out a variety of scenarios using their newly acquired abilities.

Cross-Cultural Training Component (8 Hours)

Curriculum: This is a multifaceted treatment of the Hispanic community in this country and its relationship to law enforcement and the criminal justice system. Population trends, racial characteristics, Roman law versus English law, and alien documentation are studied. Numerous subtle but important cultural barriers are explored, including deception, eye contact, differing concepts of time and direction, the Hispanic surname system, personal space and touching, and the use of the body as a personal "bank."

More in-depth presentations and discussions cover such topics as *machismo,* Hispanic women (vis-à-vis spousal abuse, domestic disturbances, rape, and incest), Hispanics and vehicular law (bribes, driving without a license or insurance, speeding, and hit-and-run), and Anglo–Hispanic stereotypes. In addition, there is a cross-cultural simulation exercise designed especially for police officers that dramatizes the problem of cultural barriers.[4]

Even with the awareness that minority populations continue to expand in the United States, the ability to communicate with them will continue to be a problem for most law enforcement agencies. Various departments are attempting to solve this problem in a number of ways. Some departments are hiring bilingual officers and offering additional compensation for their services, others maintain lists of qualified interpreters, and many agencies are including cultural awareness programs in their roll-call training.

Methods of Responding to Language Differences

An officer who arrives at the scene of a crime and is confronted by a non-English-speaking citizen must attempt to gather information from that person. In some cases, this information must not only be gathered quickly, but it must be accurate. The citizen may be a victim of a crime or a witness who can provide a description of the suspect. One of the most obvious places to turn for assistance is family or neighbors who are bilingual. By using these individuals as on-the-scene interpreters, the officer can obtain the initial information quickly. The officer should ensure that not only the name of the witness, but also the name and address of the translator, are recorded. Follow-up investigations normally utilize the services of trained translators. In some cities, the courts, prosecutors, and police agencies maintain lists of interpreters to call on if the need arises. For example, in the main Los Angeles County Courthouse, interpreters are available for 78 different languages.

It is obvious that there are inherent problems with using family or neighbors as interpreters. They may have difficulty with English, and some terms may be outside their knowledge or vocabulary. In addition, they may be biased and want to help the victim or witness, to the detriment of others. Because of these issues, departments try to utilize bilingual officers. These are officers who are able to speak and write in both English and another language. In many cases, these officers not only speak a second language, but are members of that ethnic group and are familiar with the history, traditions, and customs of the culture.

Many departments offer additional compensation to bilingual officers. Those officers respond to situations where their language skill is needed. They provide an independent interpretation without such issues as friendship or bias.

Many departments encourage roll-call training that emphasizes the cultures of minorities within their jurisdiction. This is another method by which officers may learn basic phrases of a different language. Some agencies will reimburse officers if they take and pass conversational language courses that enable them to interact with minority groups.

Other Multicultural Issues[5]

The term *culture* can be applied to various population categories. However, it is normally associated with race and ethnicity. It is this diversity that both enriches and obstructs a law enforcement officer's involvement and interaction with other persons, groups, and cultures.

Officers should remember that most minorities have developed a sharp sense for detecting condescension, manipulation, and insincerity. There is no substitute for compassion as the foundation, and sincerity as its expression, in carrying out law enforcement services equally and fairly.

Although it is not possible to feel the same compassion for all victims, it is the responsibility of law enforcement officers to provide the same compassionate service to every victim. The plight of undocumented residents or illegal aliens, for example, involves complex issues of personal prejudice and international policies. Many of these persons suffer financial exploitation and other criminal victimization once they enter the United States. Officers must make an effort to understand their situation and not let personal opinions affect their interaction with these individuals when they are victimized.

The first contact minorities have with law enforcement officers will either confirm or dispel suspicion as to how they will be treated. Proper pronunciation of a person's surname is an excellent place to begin contact with a person. Surnames have histories and meanings that allow for conversation beyond the introduction. In working with immigrant, refugee, or native populations, it is helpful to learn a few words of greeting from that culture. This willingness to go beyond what is comfortable and usual conveys the officer's intent to communicate.

Listening is fundamental to human relationships. The principles and manner of listening, however, differ among cultures. Asians and Pacific Islanders, for example, deflect direct eye contact in conversation as a sign of patient listening and deference. These groups therefore consider staring to be impolite and confrontational. Many Western cultures, on the other hand, value direct eye contact as a sign of sympathy or respect. Looking elsewhere is seen as disinterest or evasiveness. Misunderstanding in the communication process can occur if some allowance is not made for these differences. Multicultural issues must be understood by all law enforcement officers. Understanding that "different" does not mean "criminal" will assist officers attempting to communicate in an environment that continues to become more and more diverse.

COMMUNICATION WITH PERSONS WITH HEARING IMPAIRMENTS

Introduction

More than 21 million Americans suffer from some degree of hearing impairment. There is a serious problem when a law enforcement officer encounters a person who is completely deaf. The ability to communicate with such individuals is limited. Many persons with hearing impairments utilize movements of their hands, body, and face to communicate. This is known as *signing*.[6] American Sign Language, also known as *Ameslan,* is the sign language used by some deaf people in America. Many colleges and universities across the United States offer Ameslan as a course to satisfy the foreign language requirement for graduation.

Basic Principles

The interpersonal and communication skills of a police officer who contacts a deaf person will be drawn on to their fullest extent. The first and most important rule in dealing with a deaf person is never to assume he or she understands what is being communicated until positive feedback is received, either through signing or other actions.

Basic principles that officers should utilize when dealing with deaf individuals include the following:

- *Recognize that the person is deaf.* When deaf persons are approached by an officer, most will usually indicate their condition by pointing to their ears or shaking their head. The deaf person may attempt to speak, but many times the officer will not be able to understand what the person is saying. On occasion, when a deaf person attempts to speak, the speech will sound distorted. The officer should understand that this is a sign of the individual's disability and not the result of alcohol or drugs.

- *Understand the disability.* Because many deaf people rely on written communication, they may reach for a pen and paper when stopped by an officer. In some situations, such an action might be viewed as reaching for a weapon. The officer should be alert to this and not interpret the action as threatening.

- *Attempt to establish communication through any available means.* In a perfect world, the officer would understand Ameslan and be able to communicate with the deaf person. However, this is not a perfect world. The second most acceptable method of communication is through written notes. Contrary to popular belief, most deaf people do not read lips. The written notes should be clear, concise, and legible.

Use of the following phrases and their American Sign Language counterparts should enable the police officer to establish a sound working relationship with the deaf victim, suspect, or witness. After initial communication has been made, the officer can write his questions and comments or, when available and appropriate, an interpreter can be used.

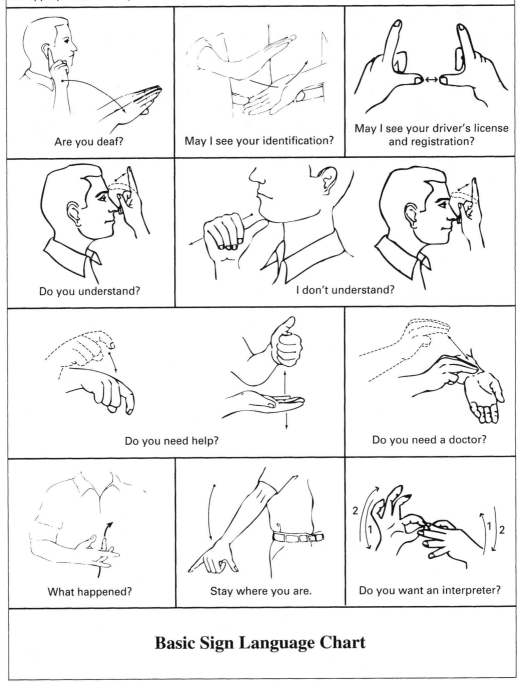

Are you deaf?

May I see your identification?

May I see your driver's license and registration?

Do you understand?

I don't understand?

Do you need help?

Do you need a doctor?

What happened?

Stay where you are.

Do you want an interpreter?

Basic Sign Language Chart

Source: "The Deaf and the Police," International Association of Chiefs of Police Training Key Series no. 244 (Alexandria, Va.).

The officer who comes into contact with a deaf person should treat that individual the same as any other person with a disability—respect, patience, and understanding will go a long way in opening lines of communication.[7] Many officers may go a number of years without coming into contact with a deaf person; however, when they do, it is essential that they understand the disability and act accordingly.

The Americans with Disabilities Act requires organizations to take all reasonable steps to accommodate those persons who have disabilities. This act is very complex and does not need an expanded discussion here. However, some public safety agencies have been sued for failing to provide adequate sign language interpreters for persons with hearing impairments. This is another example of an issue in the area of special communications that impacts officers.

Police officers, administrators, and agencies face unique communication issues in the modern world. These issues range from dealing with different cultures and languages to communicating with deaf persons. By understanding these issues and addressing them in a training environment, law enforcement personnel will be able to more effectively carry out their mission of protecting the public.

SUMMARY

Police officers and administrators face unique communication issues as law enforcement officers. The mission of law enforcement is such that these issues are rarely encountered by any other group of professionals. Officers must be aware of these special situations and strive to communicate effectively when they encounter them.

Communicating with minorities and deaf persons poses special communication needs. By becoming more sensitive to these persons' needs and backgrounds, officers will be able to communicate with them more effectively.

Negotiating with hostage takers is an unusual event for the average law enforcement officer. It should be approached with caution, but not avoided. The next chapter reviews communication in such situations.

REVIEW QUESTIONS

1. Is it realistic to expect police officers to learn a second language while attending roll-call training? Justify your answer and present any alternatives.

2. Should officers be required to learn a sign language? Why?

3. Some individuals argue that since people from other nations are in our country, they should speak our language. If you accept this principle then officers do not need to know how to communicate with other cultures. Do you agree or disagree with this position? Why?

BETTER WRITING DRILLS

In language, clarity is everything.

—Confucius

"You should say what you mean," the March Hare went on.

"I do," Alice hastily replied; "at least—at least I mean what I say—that's the same thing, you know."

"Not the same thing a bit!" said the Hatter.

"Why, you might as well say that 'I see what I eat' is the same thing as 'I eat what I see!' "

—Lewis Carroll, *Alice in Wonderland*

Choosing the Correct Word

Clear writing includes the use of correct words. As a general rule, don't use legal, technical, slang, or unfamiliar words. The overuse of certain words, such as *stated* and *advised,* also detracts from clear and concise writing. An additional characteristic of clear writing is conciseness. All unnecessary words should be left out. Details necessary in a report, however, should not be left out.

Examples

Wrong: He commenced the investigation.

Better: He started the investigation.

Wrong: The prosecutor failed to ascertain the facts necessary to prove the crime.

Better: The prosecutor failed to provide the necessary facts to prove the crime.

Wrong: The aforesaid investigation was closed.

Better: The investigation was closed.

Wrong: The victim was very pregnant.

Better: The victim was pregnant.

Wrong: He was not very often on time.

Better: He was usually late.

Wrong: There are many police officers in the city of Houston.

Better: The city of Houston has many police officers.

Are your reports clearly written? Consult this checklist for clear writing:

- In first person
- Use of active voice
- Correct use of modifiers
- Correct pronoun reference

- Use of parallelism
- Contains common words
- No unnecessary words

PRACTICAL APPLICATIONS

1. Review and practice Ameslan for three days. Attempt to carry on a conversation with other students using this sign language. Draft a report on your experiences and what you learned.

2. Correct or improve the following sentences:

   a. The police officer ran on foot after the suspect.

   b. The officer recognized him as being one Robert White.

   c. The investigation report contained information which is considered as confidential in nature.

   d. The victim was found lying in a position on her back.

   e. The accused entered the stolen vehicle and started it up.

   f. The officer opened the shotgun to see whether or not it was loaded.

   g. The room in which the crime occurred did not appear to have anything out of place. It appeared very neat.

   h. Officer would you be of assistance to me?

3. In each of the rows below, circle the correctly spelled word:

purversion	purvirsion	perversion	pervirsion
procecute	prosecute	procidute	porsecute
pneumatic	penumatic	penumatec	pnematic
pusionous	poisonous	pousuinous	poisionous
prisumptive	presumteve	presumptive	presumpative
sophesticated	sophisticated	suphisticated	suphistcated
specific	spific	spefeci	specifice
spacuious	spacous	spaciouse	spacious
stationarry	stationury	stationerry	stationary
stering	sterring	steering	steeing

4. Rewrite the following sentences as needed:

   a. The victim was very dead.

   _____

   b. The car was really on fire.

   _____

    c. This officer dismounted from his vehicle.

    _____

    d. He was not very often on time.

    _____

    e. The female officer was very pregnant.

    _____

5. Define and explain the following words or terms:

    a. signing

    _____

    b. Ameslan

    _____

    c. survival Spanish

    _____

    d. active voice

    _____

    e. passive voice

    _____

6. The following paragraph was taken from an actual police report. Make it a better paragraph.

> This officer asked Mrs. Smith if she had seen or noticed any actions that had taken place at this location at which time she responded by stating no and that she was not going to say anything else. It should be noted that Mrs. Smith appeared to be drinking and smelled like she had been drinking beer. The witness gave her name and telephone number to this officer and was released. Her name and address is appended to this report.

_____

_____

_____

_____

_____

WORDS TO KNOW

catastrophe	preliminary
cooperate	remittance
drunkenness	stated
especially	surely
female	telephone
fourteen	threat
imaginary	tortious
listen	transcript
murder	tribunal
opponent	variety

ENDNOTES

1. For an excellent article discussing cultural awareness, see Stephen M. Hennessy, "Achieving Cultural Competence," *The Police Chief* (Aug. 1993): 46.

2. Spanish is not the only language that officers will encounter. For a discussion of law enforcement agencies' experiences with Chinese, see C. Fredric Anderson and Henriettee Liu Levy, "A Guide to Chinese Names," *FBI Law Enforcement Bulletin* (Mar. 1992): 10.

3. This section is adapted from Gene B. Blair and Sam L. Slick, "Survival Spanish: Needed Training for Police," *The Police Chief* (Jan. 1990): 42–47.

4. Survival Spanish is not just a theory. Several law enforcement agencies, including the Huntsville and Austin Police Departments as well as the Georgia State Police Academy, have benefited from this type of training.

5. This section is adapted from Brian K. Ogawa, *Focus on the Future: A Prosecutor's Guide for Victim Assistance* (Washington, D.C.: National Victim Center, 1994).

6. See Jeri F. Traub, "The Hearing Impaired Individual: Suspect or Victim," in John A. Brown, Peter C. Unsinger, and Harry W. More, *Law Enforcement and Social Welfare: The Emergency Response* (Springfield, Ill.: Charles C. Thomas, 1989).

7. Robert D. Jones, "Law Enforcement and the Deaf Community," *FBI Law Enforcement Bulletin* (Nov. 1993): 18.

6

Hostage Negotiations

LEARNING OBJECTIVES

After reading this chapter, you should understand the following concepts:
- The three primary informational goals a negotiator strives for in a hostage situation.
- The relationship that develops between a negotiator and the perpetrator in a hostage situation.
- Why time is not of the essence in a hostage situation.

Unfortunately, greed, misplaced ideals, or simple incompetency can lead to situations where a criminal is placed in the position of taking an innocent party hostage. Negotiation with individuals or groups holding citizens as hostages requires special communication skills. These skills are discussed in this chapter.

INTRODUCTION

Hostage negotiation is one of the most publicized actions of law enforcement agencies, not only in the United States, but throughout the world. It is also one of the most misunderstood actions that peace officers undertake. Hostage negotiation is truly a test of the communication skills of a law enforcement officer.

On February 28, 1993, in Waco, Texas, agents of the Bureau of Alcohol, Tobacco, and Firearms (ATF) attempted to serve a search warrant on David Koresh, leader of the Branch Davidian group, at the group's compound. The raid on the compound involved more than 100 federal agents and was deemed a failure by some: four ATF agents and six Davidians died. For the next 50 days, federal agents attempted to negotiate with Koresh for his surrender. Finally, on April 19, 1993, agents fired tear gas into the compound. Within moments, the building was in flames and more than 70 sect members died inside.

The FBI was involved in a standoff at Ruby Ridge, Idaho, with Randy Weaver, an alleged white separatist. In August 1992, marshals went to Weaver's cabin to arrest him for failing to appear on a gun charge. A gunfight broke out, and Weaver's son and a federal deputy marshal were killed. The next day, Weaver's wife was accidentally shot by a federal agent as she stood unarmed in the cabin's doorway. Weaver subsequently surrendered after an 11-day standoff.

While the Davidian incident and Weaver situation may not have involved hostages in the traditional sense, both of these situations highlight the importance of communication skills during critical incidents. The Good Guys in Sacramento, the *Achille Lauro* hijacking, the bombing of TWA Flight 840, the Rome and Vienna airport attacks, and the Atlanta and Georgia prison sieges by Cuban inmates are examples of well-known hostage situations. Just listing some hostage situations brings memories of terror, death, and, in some situations, failure to save the hostages.

COMMUNICATION IN HOSTAGE SITUATIONS

The FBI classifies hostage situations in four broad categories: (1) the terrorist, (2) the prison situation, (3) the criminal, and (4) the mentally disturbed. However, the techniques utilized in each incident are the same.[1] All officers should have a fundamental understanding of hostage negotiations, since they may find themselves involved sometime in their career and because hostage negotiations are a specialized form of communication. Police administrators must also understand these principles in order to effectively supervise their departments.

Police officers are trained to take charge and control the situation. They are taught that their lives and the lives of others may depend on their ability to manage any situation. However, when those same officers are involved in a hostage negotiation situation, they must understand that their ability to completely control the events in question may be limited. The officer on the scene must attempt to contain the situation until trained negotiators arrive.

An officer's communication skills play a critical part in hostage negotiations. The officer must attempt to get the suspect to talk. The ability to communicate with the suspect is an absolute requirement in a hostage situation.

If hostage negotiators are part of a team, they should train together as often as possible.[2] This allows trust and effectiveness to build within the hostage negotiation team. All training should be evaluated and constant efforts made to improve the performance of each team member.

Training for hostage negotiators should be wide ranging, including briefings from the local telephone company on new designs and features of any communications system, and insights into personality disorders and techniques for communicating with distraught individuals from mental health professionals and members of the clergy. The department's legal advisor or the county prosecutor should discuss the legal aspects of hostage negotiations and update the members on any changes in the law. Hostage negotiators should also train by attending critiques of actual incidents.

Goals in Hostage Situations

The officer must strive for three primary informational goals in setting the stage for a successful negotiation. First, the officer must attempt to obtain specific information about the incident so the department can negotiate with the suspect on a realistic basis. The officer should attempt to determine the motivation and intent of the hostage taker through discussions with the suspect. Is the hostage taker mentally ill and suffering from delusions? Is he wanted by the police and attempting to use the hostages as leverage? Was he caught in the act of committing a crime and holding the hostages as a reaction to the situation? The answer to why the suspect is holding the hostages allows the officer to react according to the suspect's demands. The negotiator should also obtain as much information as possible about the suspect from outside sources. All of this information helps the officer find triggers to the suspect's personality and understand what personal tack to take.

Second, and similar to the first goal, the officer must attempt to gain as much information as possible from the suspect during the negotiations. The officer should not ask closed-ended questions that the hostage taker can answer with a simple yes or no. A question such as "We can't get you a million dollars, will you accept five hundred thousand?" can be answered quickly and in the positive or negative by the suspect. However, a question like "We will try to get the million, but if we can't get all of it, what else do you want?" requires explanation and engages the suspect in a discussion with the officer. In addition, this adds to the suspect's belief of being in control of the situation and able to dictate the terms of the negotiations.

The final goal of any communication effort is for the officer to express interest in what the suspect is saying. While police officers should avoid face-to-face negotiations whenever possible, the situation might arise where the officer is in close contact with the suspect.[3] The officer will want to obtain as much information as possible about the situation if there is a chance to meet with the suspect. However, the officer must also remain attentive. Verbal and nonverbal skills come into play in this situation. By maintaining eye contact with the hostage taker instead of looking around and casing the location, the officer will give the impression of being sincerely interested in what the suspect is saying. By appearing to be interested in the suspect, the officer takes the first step toward establishing a relationship with the defendant.

The relationship between the suspect and the officer who negotiates for the release of the hostages is a delicate one. The officer must appear to be professional and neutral. The suspect will realize that a hostage taker's goals and those of the officer are distinctly different, but may begin to believe that the officer can be trusted if the officer appears willing to enter into a neutral relationship for the purpose of gaining the release of the hostages. The hostage taker understands the objectives of the officer and the mission of the police, and will therefore constantly evaluate the officer's statements and actions during the negotiations. The suspect will not readily believe the officer, but will hesitantly accept the officer's role, because the suspect needs the officer in order to accomplish any goals of this action and reach an acceptable settlement.

A suspect who believes the officer is lying will not proceed with negotiations. The officer should attempt to maintain credibility by agreeing to only those demands that the suspect could reasonably be expected to accept. For example, the officer should not agree to give the suspect the Hope diamond. However, the officer might be able to convince the suspect that several one-carat diamonds could be obtained. Open and credible communication between the officer and the suspect leads to the beginning of a relationship. The officer has taken the first step toward establishing that relationship when he and the suspect can rationally discuss alternatives.

Time is not of the essence in hostage negotiations. Just the reverse—the officer should do everything possible to consume time. From a tactical perspective, the longer the negotiations take, the more likely the suspect is to make an error that will lead to apprehension.

The lapse of time allows the officer to establish a relationship with the hostage taker. One technique is to explain to the suspect that all requests must be cleared by headquarters. This allows for a delay between receiving a request and having to act on it.

Delaying the negotiation will wear down the suspect. The passage of time requires the suspect to continue to watch the hostages, anticipate police responses to demands, and worry about the consequences of these actions. This stress on the hostage taker may allow the officer to negotiate a deal. It should be obvious, however, that this can be a two-edged sword, in that stress may also cause the suspect to act irrationally and harm one of the hostages. The officer must be able to anticipate the suspect's moods and intentions and react accordingly.

In the best of all possible worlds the officer should be able to offer the suspect a deal in which it appears to the hostage taker that both parties win. A win–win solution is very hard to achieve. Hostage negotiation is simply a bargaining process in which each side has a bottom line. Most negotiations center on moving from stated unrealistic demands to finding appropriate points of agreement. The negotiator must attempt to steer the suspect's demands away from absolutes to acceptance of certain realistic demands in exchange for other alternatives. For example, in a situation where a hostage needs medical attention, the negotiator may obtain the release of that hostage in return for a minor concession in another area, such as giving the suspect special food. This bargaining process is part of establishing a relationship between the suspect and the officer.

Many negotiators do not believe offering the suspect access to a radio or television is a wise tactical decision. They like to cut suspects off from the outside world and therefore make them more dependent on the negotiator. Additionally, news media coverage of the situation might impair negotiations.

Normally, the officer is replaced by trained negotiators during the incident. However, the officer must be prepared to carry out all the negotiations if no other trained personnel are available and must be ready to accept the suspect's surrender at any time. If the suspect indicates a desire to surrender, the officer must communicate the procedure in a clear, professional manner that is reassuring to the suspect. If, as part of the surrender, certain concessions or agreements with the suspect were made, the officer should endeavor to abide by them whenever practical. For example, if the officer agreed to allow the suspect to meet with a representative of the media, that agreement should, if possible, be honored. The purpose of honoring such agreements is simple—other potential hostage takers will understand that the police keep their promises in such situations.

Guidelines for Negotiation[4]

- Stablilize and contain the situation.
- Select the right time to make contact.
- Take your time when negotiating.
- Allow the subject to speak; it is more important to be a good listener than a good talker.
- Don't offer the subject anything.
- Be as honest as possible; avoid tricks.
- Never dismiss any request as trivial.
- Never say "no."
- Soften the demands.
- Never set a deadline; try not to accept a deadline. If a deadline is set, let it pass without comment if possible.
- Do not make alternative suggestions.
- Do not introduce outsiders (non–law enforcement) into the negotiation process.
- Do not allow any exchange of hostages; especially do not exchange a negotiator for a hostage.
- Avoid negotiating face to face.

Profile of Hostage Negotiation Teams[5]

In February 1992, hostage negotiators and members of special operations teams gathered to exchange information and experiences. There is little comprehensive data regarding hostage negotiation activities in the United States. Therefore, members attending the February conference agreed to complete a survey to learn more about the needs of hostage negotiation teams.

The survey was a 44-page questionnaire asking specific questions regarding issues that affect negotiation teams. The survey was based on input from FBI hostage negotiators. The survey was reviewed by those negotiators, as well as other experts, to ensure its accuracy.

The survey revealed that very few females served on hostage negotiation teams. The ethnic composition of the teams was primarily white. Most team members were assigned to investigation or patrol, with some in administration. Only 41 percent of those surveyed stated that their department had any written negotiator selection policy. Once selected to serve on a hostage negotiation team, very few of the members received more than 10 days of training. Once a team member, the amount of training did not improve. The majority of team members received less than 5 days of inservice training each year.

This survey points out the importance of effective communication in hostage situations. Many hostage negotiation teams may have very little training in crisis management; therefore, the ability to communicate with the perpetrator becomes critical. Failure to communicate effectively may have deadly results.

The Critical Incident Negotiation Team

In 1985, the Crisis Management Unit at the FBI Academy established the Critical Incident Negotiation Team (CINT).[6] This team is a small, highly trained, and mobile group of experienced FBI negotiators. The FBI negotiates approximately 45 bank robbery and hijacking hostage incidents each year. The original CINT members were selected from more than 350 FBI agents nationwide on the basis of law enforcement background, personal interviews, psychological testing, and negotiation experience. Twenty-five negotiators were selected. The Crisis Management Unit arranged and coordinated semiannual training seminars for team members.

The FBI deploys CINT negotiators both within and outside the boundaries of the United States. Negotiators have been used at Ruby Ridge, Idaho; Waco, Texas; and in other high-profile, emotionally charged situations. Additionally, negotiators have assisted in the release of American hostages held in Ecuador, Chile, El Salvador, and other countries.

CINT negotiators are also engaged in training international police forces. They have met with police forces around the world to provide training in crisis management as it pertains to kidnapping and hostage incidents.

Protracted hostage situations require special skill and training. The FBI Critical Incident Negotiation Team is one federal agency's response to this demand. Training and consultation may prevent the loss of innocent lives in such a situation.

SUMMARY

Hostage negotiation is one of the most difficult situations any officer will have to face. It involves tact, understanding, and patience. More important, it requires all of the officer's communication skills. All police officers should be familiar with the communication skills involved in hostage negotiations. The officer on patrol may have to begin and carry out such negotiations while waiting for specially trained negotiators to arrive at the scene.

REVIEW QUESTIONS

1. What are the personal characteristics of a good negotiator?
2. At what point in a hostage situation should the negotiator call for armed intervention instead of negotiations?
3. How much training should hostage negotiation teams receive?

PRACTICAL APPLICATIONS

1. Rank the following types of training in order of importance for members of a newly formed hostage negotiation team:

   Lecture on use of force

   Firearms training

   Hand-to-hand combat training

   Lecture on communication techniques

   Lecture on the law of search and seizure

   Sensitivity training

   Introduction to psychology

2. List the equipment hostage negotiation team members should carry in their car when responding to a crisis. Assume they can carry a package no larger than what airlines allow passengers to carry onto a plane.

3. In each of the rows below, circle the correctly spelled word:

tempareture	tamperature	temperature	temperatuer
tranpese	trenspose	tranpose	transpose
traecherous	treacherous	treachous	trecaher
transeint	tranient	tranisent	transient
transquil	transquile	tranquil	tranquile
porngraphic	pronrographic	pronogaphic	pornographic
puntive	punetive	punitive	puniteve
quarantine	quaranetine	quarentive	quaranteve
quareled	quarrele	quarreled	quared
quato	quata	queta	quota

4. Rewrite the following sentences as needed:

   a. Having a lot of work to do, he arrived earlier.

   _____

   b. The criminal left his fingerprints at the scene, this officer found several of them.

   _____

   c. The defendant appeared in court and he acted nervously.

   _____

   d. This officer shot the pistol four times and cleaned it.

   _____

e. The offender was finally booked and this officer went home.

_____

5. Define and explain the following words or terms:
   a. hostage negotiation

   _____

   b. critical incident negotiation team

   _____

   c. Branch Davidian incident

   _____

   d. prison hostage situation

   _____

   e. terrorist hostage situation

   _____

6. The following paragraph was taken from an actual police report. Make it a better paragraph.

   When I arrived at the location of the victim's home, the victim, Bill Brown stated that he discovered that his television set was stolen from his home. Before leaving he locked all his doors and windows and returned only 20 minutes later. He claimed that person or persons unknown may have entered his home at some time during the last day and that he only missed the television set.

   _____

   _____

   _____

   _____

   _____

WORDS TO KNOW

barricade	negotiate
demand	surrender
emotional	trade
money	utilities

ENDNOTES

1. See G. Dwayne Fuselier and Gary W. Noesner, "Confronting the Terrorist Hostage Taker," *FBI Law Enforcement Bulletin* (July 1990): 6.

2. John L. Grey, "Keeping Crisis Negotiations Skills Sharp," *Law and Order* (Sept. 1994): 177.

3. There appears to be a split among the authorities on the issue of negotiating face-to-face with the hostage taker. One of the FBI guidelines for negotiation listed in the focus box is to avoid negotiating face to face. The International Association of Chiefs of Police, in their *Training Key* Series no. 235 (Alexandria, Va.), indicate that the officer should maintain eye contact when meeting with the suspect.

4. G. Dwayne Fuselier and Gray W. Noesner, "Confronting the Terrorist Hostage Taker," *FBI Law Enforcement Bulletin* (July 1990).

5. This section is adapted from Mitchell R. Hammer, Clinton R. Van Zandt, and Randall G. Rogan, "Crisis/Hostage Negotiation Team Profile," *FBI Law Enforcement Bulletin* (Mar. 1994): 9.

6. This section is adapted from J. M. Botting, F. J. Lanceley, and G. W. Noesner, "The FBI's Critical Incident Negotiation Team," *FBI Law Enforcement Bulletin* (Apr. 1995): 12–15.

7

Communicating in Public

LEARNING OBJECTIVE

After reading this chapter, you should understand the following concepts:
- How to draft a speech.
- How to present a speech.
- The different types of media and their objectives.
- How to conduct an interview with the media.
- The rules that apply to media access to crime scenes.

KEY TERMS

Sidebar story—An article that is placed in a column next to the main article in a newspaper.

Public affairs officer—The police department's official point of contact with the media.

> ### Law Enforcement and the Media
>
> Who can forget the almost gavel-to-gavel coverage of the O.J. Simpson murder trial? There were television pictures of the scene of the crime, the now-famous live coverage of the Bronco traveling the L.A. freeways, the interviews with prosecution and defense attorneys, and the courtroom drama that became almost a daily soap opera for millions of Americans.

The media have the ability to bring crime into our living rooms. It is therefore critical for law enforcement officers to understand how the media work and how to communicate with them effectively. We talk with friends and colleagues on a daily basis, and although this is a form of communicating in the public arena, there are distinct differences between this and giving a speech or being interviewed by the local television station. This chapter examines some techniques that can facilitate a law enforcement officer's ability to effectively communicate in public situations.

PUBLIC SPEAKING

Most criminal justice professionals will be called on sometime in their careers to make presentations to the general public. This may be an informal gathering of citizens at a Neighborhood Watch meeting or a formal presentation to the city council. Many officers suffer from stage fright when speaking to groups. As with any other skill, practice makes perfect. This is not to say all of us will become dynamic and forceful speakers. Some people are better than others at appearing and communicating in public. However, if certain basic and simple procedures are mastered, any officer can make a creditable presentation.

Preparing for the Speech

Some of the bravest officers become quivering masses of jelly at the thought of facing a group of citizens and explaining simple law enforcement concepts. We talk to other persons all the time. Public speaking is simply talking to more than one person. However, once we move into a group setting, the rules of communication change. Feedback may be delayed or never received. We may have physical barriers, such as a nonworking microphone, that prevent those in the back of the room from hearing us. Add to this the typical worry of making a mistake or looking unprofessional and many of us dread speaking in public.

Drafting the Speech

The thought of having to stand up and present a speech to a room full of people can be very intimidating, and writing a speech can be an agonizing task for many law enforcement officers. However, a speech should be prepared differently from a term paper or a departmental position paper. Some simple rules follow for writing your speech:

1. *Prepare an outline of the topics you want to discuss.* Start with your main objective or theme. The first thing to write down is what you want the audience to do as the result of the speech. Keep this objective in mind while writing the rest of the speech.

2. *Draft an outline of the main points you want to discuss.* There should be only three or four major items on the list. If you have a laundry list of items, think about combining them or rethink what it is you want to accomplish with the speech.

3. *Revise the outline several times.* Then begin to add additional information to your main points. Think about each piece of information that you are adding. Does it explain your main point?

4. *Remember, we write differently than we speak.* Practice your speech by speaking it out loud. Based on several rehearsals, you may want to revise your presentation.

5. *Prepare an outline and deliver your speech based on the outline.* You should know the subject matter well enough beforehand so that you need only refer to the outline instead of a long typewritten speech. Your delivery will be more natural.

6. *When writing a speech, start at the middle or end.* The most difficult part of a speech is the opening. This should be done last.

Once your speech is written, the next step is to deliver it. The following section briefly examines some simple principles that can make public presentations more professional for law enforcement officers.

Some Dos and Don'ts of Public Speaking

There are as many rules for effective public speaking as there are dynamic speakers.[1] No one approach will work for all persons. This is not a text on public speaking, nor is it our intent to include a great deal of detail on the various techniques of effective speaking. However, there are several simple, easily mastered methods that will allow most officers to make clear and meaningful presentations. The following rules will assist in making oral presentations:

1. *Understand the topic of your speech.* What does the group expect to hear? If they want to be informed about the patrol functions of the department, don't deliver a speech on the records division.
2. *Know your audience and direct your speech to their interests and knowledge level.* Nothing is more boring than a speech full of technical jargon that the audience doesn't understand. Talk on their level and the reward will be an interested audience.
3. *Humor is excellent, but it can backfire.* If you are comfortable, humor can break the ice and relax the audience for the speech. However, a long, drawn-out joke that does not go over with the audience leaves a bad taste with everyone.
4. *Always be on time and dress appropriately.* Common courtesy requires that you do not keep the audience waiting for your arrival. Know the exact starting time and show up a few minutes early.
5. *Do not read your speech word for word.* We have all sat through public speeches where the speaker droned on and on reading from prepared notes.
6. *Understand how long you are expected to speak and ensure that you do not go over that time limit.* Even if you think you have the audience eating out of the palm of your hand, do not prolong the speech. Remember, the group may have other business, and if you are that good, they will ask you to return.
7. *Whenever possible, use visual aids.* Nothing makes your point as well as visual aids. Businesses have known this for years. We in the public sector should take the hint and use visual aids whenever possible.
8. *Rehearse as many times as your work schedule will allow.* Rehearse, rehearse, rehearse, especially during the beginning of your public speaking career.

9. *Ask for honest feedback from the person who asked you to make the speech.* Don't simply say, "How was I?" This will lead to the standard response, "You were great." Politely press the person to offer comments on how you could make the presentation better the next time. It's amazing that, once encouraged to give feedback, many people will provide helpful suggestions on how to make a presentation more effective.

Public speaking is really more of an art than a science, but by following the preceding rules any officer can become a better public speaker.

Speaking to a group of citizens or elected officials requires certain techniques. However, different rules apply when attempting to communicate with the media. The next section examines this important aspect of law enforcement communications.

COMMUNICATION WITH THE MEDIA

Unfortunately, many police officers, administrators, and chiefs view news reporters with distrust.[2] Just as the police have a mission to accomplish, so do the media. The Constitution prohibits the federal and state governments from passing any law that abridges the freedom of the press. The media call this *the people's right to know.* The striving by the media to inform the public occasionally conflicts with a law enforcement agency's desire to keep certain information confidential. Only by understanding the media and their role in society can an administrator work effectively with them to present the department's position.

Relations with the Media

Understanding the media must begin with a clarification of the different types of media. The law enforcement administrator must understand that certain basic fundamental principles apply to the media in general. In addition, distinct rules, goals, and standards pertain to different types of media.

Law enforcement agencies interact with three basic types of media: (1) newspapers, (2) radio, and (3) television.

Newspapers Newspapers usually provide more in-depth coverage than the electronic media. In addition, many newspapers are interested in the human aspects of a story. As will be discussed, electronic media must use short and to-the-point stories. Newspapers may run a major story coupled with a sidebar story that touches on another aspect of the main story. A *sidebar story* is usually an article that is placed in a column next to the main article. Many newspapers will assign a full-time police or court reporter. This reporter will know the officers, the language of the streets, and the law nearly as well as any police officer.

Radio A radio broadcast carries only the officer's voice. Radio reporters do not have to capture the scene with pictures; therefore, many interviews with the police are conducted over the telephone. Many radio stations have hourly newscasts and can therefore update the public more effectively than newspapers, which are published daily, or television, which has evening or nightly newscasts. In this day of visual media, an effective administrator should not overlook radio as a means by which the public may be informed of the department's activities.

Television This is the medium we are most familiar with. It brings the action right into our living rooms as it occurs. Many of us have watched from the comfort of our easy chairs as hostage scenes and riots happen. Television is visual by its very nature. A simple news release does not satisfy the television director, who wants and needs pictures: a uniformed officer speaking, a suspect being placed in a patrol vehicle, the front of a shot-up building. These types of graphic scenes are what television is searching for daily. In addition, television news is short and to the point. Normally, a story on the evening news is 20 to 30 seconds in length. No matter how long the reporter interviews an officer, the final broadcast will usually run no longer than one minute.

Understanding the distinctions between the different types of media allows the law enforcement administrator to deal with them in an effective manner. Chiefs, administrators, and officers will have contact with the media—sometimes on a daily basis. Many departments have codified the rules for these contacts by distributing an SOP on media relations. This procedure has several advantages. First, it assures the media and the city manager that there is uniformity in dealing with the press. Second, it establishes procedures that both parties know and can follow. If media representatives are consulted when the document is being drafted, they will be more understanding of its purpose and will follow the procedures more readily. Finally, the SOP informs the officers on the street how they should respond to an unexpected contact with a news reporter.

Using a public affairs officer (PAO) is becoming more common in law enforcement agencies.[3] A PAO is the department's official point of contact with the media. There are several different approaches to utilizing a PAO. One approach is to make the public affairs officer the official spokesperson for the department. All interviews are conducted by the PAO. While this approach may provide continuity, it is not the most effective method of dealing with either the public or the media. Any top-level administrator who has above-average communication skills should be able to conduct a live interview with the media.

A second approach is to establish the position as an official assignment and rotate officers through it based on their experience, intelligence, and ability. This alternative allows the public and media to talk to a sworn officer. The disadvantage is that, depending on the length of the assignment, the media will have to readjust to a new officer every time there is a rotation of officers.

Many top-level administrators have experienced sleepless nights over leaks to the press by members of their department. News reporters are ethically bound not to reveal the identity of their sources. Just as police officers will not reveal the names of their confidential reliable informants, so do news reporters carefully guard the identity of their sources. Some states have *shield laws* that prevent a news reporter from being held in contempt of court for refusing to comply with a court order to reveal the name of a source. In addition, there have been numerous incidents of reporters going to jail rather than giving up the identity of their sources. By accepting the fact that occasionally there will be leaks to the media, the effective administrator should attempt to work out a relationship with the press that minimizes the impact of a leak. On occasion, an officer may promise to keep the media informed if they will withhold the story until the appropriate time. Another technique is to appeal to the integrity of the reporter and explain the consequences of releasing the story. It is fruitless to get angry at the reporter or the unnamed source. Human nature being what it is, leaks will continue as long as there is a reporter willing to listen.

Effective media relations should include conferences between the chief or a designated representative, the news director of the television or radio station, and the editor or publisher of the newspaper. These periodic conferences can sometimes be stormy, but they allow each party to understand the other's point of view. This relationship is especially helpful if the department is on the receiving end of a story that is critical of the agency. Media representatives should always attempt to contact the department for its side before the story is run. In the event that a reporter neglects to reach the department, a call to the editor will usually provide the opportunity for a follow-up story on the department's position.

Establishing an ongoing relationship with the media is a necessary function of any law enforcement administrator. It must always be based on trust and mutual respect. Once such a relationship has been created, it will benefit both the department and the public.

Preparing for and Conducting the Interview

Understanding the goal of the media assists the officer in preparing for and conducting an interview. The first few times an officer or administrator participates in a media interview can be frightening. When the newspaper reporter begins to take notes, or the radio or TV reporter thrusts a microphone at the officer, it is an overpowering experience.

Preparation before the interview can help calm the officer's nerves. Being knowledgeable about the facts of the incident, as well as of the agency's position, can enhance communication. If there are photo opportunities available, ensure that the media are made aware of them. Never, never lie or distort the truth. The officer's credibility and that of the department are on the line. An officer who doesn't have an answer should say so and offer to find out. If the promise is made, ensure that it is kept.

Once the officer has reviewed the facts and had preliminary discussions with the media, the actual interview will take place. By this time it may seem anticlimactic. Remember to speak clearly in everyday language and avoid the use of jargon. "I observed the defendant committing a 211 and responded over the net with a 10-14" does not tell the public or the media representative what really occurred. "I saw the suspect fleeing from the convenience store with a gun in his hand and believed he had committed a robbery. I radioed for assistance and was able to arrest the suspect two blocks away" is a more complete statement.

If the officer is anxious about talking to a reporter because of being seen on the nightly news by thousands of citizens, it is sometimes helpful to remember that this is a one-on-one conversation. The camera is recording only what is said between the officer and the reporter. On occasion an officer will be called on to give an interview "live" instead of taped, edited, and replayed at a later time. The officer should approach this situation in the same manner as with a taped interview. Be professional and communicate clearly with the reporter, not the unseen masses.

Relations with the media have traditionally been tense. By understanding the purposes and working conditions of media representatives and trying to assist them whenever possible, an officer or administrator may become an effective spokesperson for the department. This, in turn, will make the job of policing the community easier when the public understands the agency's position.

Media Access to Crime Scenes

As indicated previously, there has historically been a state of distrust between the media and law enforcement. One of the areas that causes the most friction is media access to crime scenes.[4] The media argue that the public's right to know should allow them special privileges, including unrestricted access to crime scenes. Law enforcement's position is that unrestricted access by the media may contaminate the scene of a crime.

This conflict may have been resolved in a series of three U.S. Supreme Court decisions that establish the parameters of the media's First Amendment newsgathering privilege.[5] The Supreme Court stated that the right of media to access information held by law enforcement is no greater than that of the general public and that law enforcement can prevent the media from obtaining access to information or areas not generally available to the public.

Different rules apply once the media acquires information. The courts have held that almost all attempts to prevent the media from publishing information will fail. This concept is known as *prior restraint*.[6] The Supreme Court has stated that only governmental allegation and proof that publication must inevitably, directly, and immediately cause the occurrence of an event kindred to imperiling the safety of a transport at sea can support the issuance of an interim restraining order.[7]

The media are driven by both First Amendment concerns and simple business issues of scooping other members of the press. Law enforcement officers must protect crime scenes and conduct criminal investigations. There will be continuing conflict between the media and law enforcement regarding access to crime scenes. Simply understanding this conflict will allow law enforcement officers to act accordingly.

SUMMARY

Public speaking, like any other skill, requires practice. During the early phase of any law enforcement officer's career, speeches will be more informal. However, as an officer rises up the promotion ladder, the nature of the speaking engagements will change and more formal rules of presentation will be required. Just as we learn to adapt to changing work environments, so must we learn to tailor our speeches to different types of audiences.

The media is not an enemy to be attacked or avoided. The efficient administrator will become familiar with the different types of media and their specific needs. While there will always be tension between the media's search for the truth and the police department's requirement to keep certain information confidential, each party can learn to respect the other and work toward a common goal of providing service to the general public.

REVIEW QUESTIONS

1. What is the most difficult aspect of public speaking?
2. What makes one speaker more dynamic than others? List specific characteristics that you believe are essential to effective public speaking.
3. Is there any occasion that you can think of when a senior administrator should become a source for a news reporter?

BETTER WRITING DRILLS

Officers sometimes observe, use, or seize foreign currency. While it is not practical to memorize all foreign currency denominations, some of the more commonly encountered types of foreign money are listed in the following table. Similar to the drill in Chapter 2, the country is listed in one column and the basic monetary unit is listed next to it. Try to determine the name of the foreign money and then check your results.

COUNTRY OR AREA	BASIC MONETARY UNIT
Argentina	Peso
Bolivia	Peso Boliviana
Canada	Dollar
Ecuador	Sucre
Honduras	Lempira
Italy	Lira
Laos	Kip
Mexico	Peso
Pakistan	Rupee

PRACTICAL APPLICATIONS

1. Select five classmates and have each present a three-minute speech. Discuss how the speech could have been improved. What is the most common mistake made by all the students?

2. Watch five television news shows where police officers are interviewed. If you were the officer, what changes or modifications to that officer's statements would you make? Why?

3. Using those same television shows, draft questions you would have asked the officer if you were the reporter.

4. In each of the rows below, circle the correctly spelled word:

taurama	tauram	trama	trauma
trespasing	trespassing	tresspasing	trespessing
tunge	tounge	tounge	tongue
typwritter	typwriter	typewriter	typewrited
tobacco	tabacco	tobaccoo	tobaco
vormin	vernim	vernin	vermin
vandelism	vandelism	vandelesm	vandalism
vareity	variety	varetiy	varietty
vehecle	veihile	vehicle	veichle
usualy	unualluy	unsually	unusually
urene	urini	uirine	urine

5. Rewrite the following sentences as needed:

a. Jerry and her smoked marijuana.

b. My partner and me made four arrests last week.

_____

c. Dave and myself found the gun.

_____

d. I run to the hurt victim.

_____

e. He did not know that the police was aware of him's conduct.

_____

6. Define and explain the following words or terms:
   a. sidebar story

   _____

   b. media access

   _____

   c. position paper

   _____

   d. PAO

   _____

   e. the people's right to know

   _____

7. The following paragraph was taken from an actual police report. Make it a better paragraph.

   This officer responded to the location of the parking lot of the liquor store and upon arrival saw two male subjects staring each other as if they wanted to fight each other or someone else. This officer exited the police vehicle and upon doing so subject Davis turned, dropped his weapon, and ran eastbound through the alley. At this time this officer's partner responded to subject Smith who was standing at the location and this officer yelled at subject Davis to freeze and to return to this officer.

   _____

   _____

   _____

   _____

WORDS TO KNOW

ache	minority
athletics	nuisance
business	permanent
complainant	quiet
desperate	respond
existence	thought
fulfill	traumatic
immediately	unanimous
lenient	vacancy
maintenance	writing

ENDNOTES

1. For an excellent discussion of public speaking, see Steven N. Bowman, "The Practical Local Government Manager," *Public Administration* (Dec. 1991): 22–23.

2. Some of this mistrust is based on law enforcement's perception of how the media reports crime; see Steven M. Chermak, "Body Count News: How Crime Is Presented in the News Media," *Justice Quarterly* 11, no. 4 (Dec. 1994): 561.

3. See Craig A. Sullivan, "Police Public Relations," *Law and Order* (Oct. 1993): 94, for a discussion of how one agency interacts with the media.

4. Kimberly A. Crawford, "News Media Participation in Law Enforcement Activities," *FBI Law Enforcement Bulletin* (Aug. 1994): 29.

5. See *Branzburg v. Hayes,* 408 U.S. 665 (1972); *Houchins v. KQED,* 438 U.S. 1 (1977); and *Press-Enterprise Co. v. Superior Court of California,* 106 S.Ct. 2735 (1986).

6. *New York Times Co. v. United States,* 403 U.S. 713 (1971).

7. Ibid.

8

Law Enforcement Records

LEARNING OBJECTIVES

After reading this chapter, you should understand the following concepts:
- The objectives of any law enforcement records system.
- The areas within a police department that can be made more effective by using computers.
- The media's position regarding access to police records.

Any decision made in a law enforcement agency is, or should be, based on the evaluation of all available information. Information or data is located in several places: an individual's memory, written works, or electronic storage. The law enforcement agency's records division is the primary location for all related information on which police officers base their operational and administrative decisions. All authorities in the field of police report writing agree that an efficient and effective records section is an essential part of the planning and execution of operations.[1]

Law enforcement records systems vary from city to city and serve different purposes depending on the level or responsibility of the agency. Records for a local police department will be different from those maintained by a federal agency. However, certain basic principles should remain the same no matter where the agency is located or at what level it operates.

CRIMINAL JUSTICE RECORDS SYSTEMS

Any records system should incorporate certain standard criteria into its operation. Scholars and authorities in the field recommend the following two standards as a minimum:

1. Consolidation of all records into one division. This allows for centralization of authority and responsibility within the department. One administrator should be responsible for this division.
2. Standardization of all records and reporting systems within an agency. This provides for ease of administration and ensures the proper reporting of all necessary information.

Adoption of these standards will ensure that a records system is operational. Additionally, any valid police records system should allow the police administrator to carry out certain tasks. The following 14 functions are critical objectives of any records system:

1. Ascertain the nature and extent of crime within the jurisdiction of the agency.
2. Update the staffing level of the department.
3. Provide a means to control the reporting and investigation of crimes.
4. Arrest offenders by analysis of their modus operandi.
5. Report and analyze traffic accidents with the objective of working with other city departments to correct dangerous intersections or roads.
6. Follow up on arrests and the disposition of cases.
7. Predict trends in crime to maximize the use of law enforcement personnel by properly deploying them to the areas of greatest need.
8. Detect unusual trends within the department and the community.
9. Assist in the assignment and promotion of personnel.
10. Provide information for use in criminal investigations.
11. Ascertain the level and maintenance of police equipment.
12. Predict future trends in criminal activity.
13. Prepare the department's annual budget.
14. Provide information to citizens and elected officials regarding matters of concern.

Police records systems must ensure that any communication is clearly understandable. Most operational and administrative communication takes the final form of written documents. Written documents are preferable to oral statements because there is less chance for misunderstanding in a properly drafted document. Additionally, written reports, orders, or policies allow members of the police force to refer to the document if there is any question concerning its application, effect, or content. Written documents may take many forms.

Some law enforcement agencies combine oral statements with written reports. Patrol officers in the St. Louis County Police Department telephone headquarters and orally report to a trained specialist. The information is entered on a preformatted computer system that electronically processes the report.[2]

However, the mere collection of data or information without subsequent action does not assist a department in carrying out its mission. The following section examines how certain types of police records are processed.

PROCESSING OF REPORTS

Processing police reports in a timely and accurate manner is one of the most important functions of the records division.[3] This section gives a brief overview of using computers to process certain types of reports.

A police department, by its very nature, generates a large number of reports. These reports are normally stored in the records division. Without an efficient sys-

HARRISBURG POLICE BUREAU

FIELD TRAINING AND EVALUATION PROGRAM

DAILY OBSERVATION REPORT

Recruits Last Name, First Initial   Badge No.   F.T.O. Last Name, First Initial   Badge No.   Date MM/DD/YY

Assignment or Reason for no Evaluation:_____

RATING INSTRUCTIONS: Use below scale to rate trainee. Comment on any category you wish. However, <u>SPECIFIC</u> comments <u>MUST</u> be made on the reverse side if a rating of 1,2,6, or 7 is indicated <u>OR</u> if "Failure to respond to training" is indicated. During Phase IV comments <u>MUST</u> be made on all ratings except a 4.

Rating Scale-------------Not Acceptable   Acceptable   Exceptional
(circle most appropriate)   1   2   3   4   5   6   7

	Rating	None Observed	Remedial Training (Time)	Responding To Training
APPEARANCE				
1. General Appearance --	1 2 3 4 5 6 7	☐		YES☐ NO☐
ATTITUDE				
2. Toward Police Work and Criticism -----------------------------	1 2 3 4 5 6 7	☐		YES☐ NO☐
KNOWLEDGE				
3. Knowledge of Bureau Policies and Procedures ------------------	1 2 3 4 5 6 7	☐		YES☐ NO☐
4. Knowledge of Rules of Criminal Procedure ----------------------	1 2 3 4 5 6 7	☐		YES☐ NO☐
5. Knowledge of Crimes Code (Title 18) ---------------------------	1 2 3 4 5 6 7	☐		YES☐ NO☐
6. Knowledge of Vehicle Code (Title 75) --------------------------	1 2 3 4 5 6 7	☐		YES☐ NO☐
7. Knowledge of City Ordinances ---------------------------------	1 2 3 4 5 6 7	☐		YES☐ NO☐
PERFORMANCE				
8. Driving Skill: Normal, Moderate, High Stress Conditions -----------	1 2 3 4 5 6 7	☐		YES☐ NO☐
9. Knowledge of City Geography / Response Time to Calls ----------	1 2 3 4 5 6 7	☐		YES☐ NO☐
10. Report Writing: Accuracy, Timeliness, Grammar, Spelling, etc. ----	1 2 3 4 5 6 7	☐		YES☐ NO☐
11. Field Performance: Stress / Non-Stress Situations ---------------	1 2 3 4 5 6 7	☐		YES☐ NO☐
12. Investigative Skills: Interview and Interrogation ----------------	1 2 3 4 5 6 7	☐		YES☐ NO☐
13. Self Initiated Field Activity --------------------------------------	1 2 3 4 5 6 7	☐		YES☐ NO☐
14 Officer Safety: General, Susp. Person, Voice and Physical Skills ---	1 2 3 4 5 6 7	☐		YES☐ NO☐
15. Problem Solving and Decision Making --------------------------	1 2 3 4 5 6 7	☐		YES☐ NO☐
16. Radio: Listens-Comprehends and Articulates Transmissions ------	1 2 3 4 5 6 7	☐		YES☐ NO☐
RELATIONSHIPS				
17. With Citizens in General and other Ethnic Groups ---------------	1 2 3 4 5 6 7	☐		YES☐ NO☐

TRAINEE'S NAME (PRINT)   Badge No.   Date MM/DD/YY

Acknowledgement of review of this evaluation report

Harrisburg Police Bureau Daily Observation Report. An example of a small agency's reporting form. *(Courtesy of Chief Richard Shaffer, Harrisburg, Pennsylvania Bureau of Police.)*

VANCOUVER POLICE DEPARTMENT
INVESTIGATION REPORT

BULLETIN | CRIME INFO | FILE

FILE NO.

INCIDENT NO.

1005 (87)-A

PAGE _____ OF _____

SECTION 1 — OCCURRENCE INFORMATION

1. LOCATION	TEAM AREA	2. DATE OF OCCURRENCE	TIME
		FROM:	
3. OFFENCE / OCCURRENCE	VPD CODE	TO:	
	UCR CODE	4. DATE INVESTIGATED	

PERSONS CODE   V - VICTIM   R - REPORTEE   P - PARENT / GUARDIAN   W - WITNESS   CIRCLE APPLICABLE CODE

#1

5. NAME (SNME, G1, G2 OR BUSINESS NAME)						LANGUAGE ASSISTANCE		STATEMENT YES ☐ NO ☐	VWSU CARD

V | RACE | SEX | D.O.B. | AGE | HEIGHT | WEIGHT | HAIR | EYE | UTL. ALCH. ☐ DRUG ☐ | TOURIST
R | RES. ADDRESS (NO. DIR. NAME, TYPE, APT/STE, CITY) | | POSTAL CODE | RES. PHONE | I.D. TYPE-NUMBER
P |
W | BUS. ADDRESS | BUS. PHONE | OCCUPATION | WORK HOURS

#2

6. NAME (SNME, G1, G2 OR BUSINESS NAME)						LANGUAGE ASSISTANCE		STATEMENT YES ☐ NO ☐	VWSU CARD

V | RACE | SEX | D.O.B. | AGE | HEIGHT | WEIGHT | HAIR | EYE | UTL. ALCH. ☐ DRUG ☐ | TOURIST
R | RES. ADDRESS (NO. DIR. NAME, TYPE, APT/STE, CITY) | | POSTAL CODE | RES. PHONE | I.D. TYPE-NUMBER
P |
W | BUS. ADDRESS | BUS. PHONE | OCCUPATION | WORK HOURS

#3

7. NAME (SNME, G1, G2 OR BUSINESS NAME)						LANGUAGE ASSISTANCE		STATEMENT YES ☐ NO ☐	VWSU CARD

V | RACE | SEX | D.O.B. | AGE | HEIGHT | WEIGHT | HAIR | EYE | UTL. ALCH. ☐ DRUG ☐ | TOURIST
R | RES. ADDRESS (NO. DIR. NAME, TYPE, APT/STE, CITY) | | POSTAL CODE | RES. PHONE | I.D. TYPE-NUMBER
P |
W | BUS. ADDRESS | BUS. PHONE | OCCUPATION | WORK HOURS

#4

8. NAME (SNME, G1, G2 OR BUSINESS NAME)						LANGUAGE ASSISTANCE		STATEMENT YES ☐ NO ☐	VWSU CARD

V | RACE | SEX | D.O.B. | AGE | HEIGHT | WEIGHT | HAIR | EYE | UTL. ALCH. ☐ DRUG ☐ | TOURIST
R | RES. ADDRESS (NO. DIR. NAME, TYPE, APT/STE, CITY) | | POSTAL CODE | RES. PHONE | I.D. TYPE-NUMBER
P |
W | BUS. ADDRESS | BUS. PHONE | OCCUPATION | WORK HOURS

INJURED PERSON   ENTER APPLICABLE PERSONS CODE AND NUMBER

CODE	9. TAKEN TO	10. TRANSPORTED BY	11. DESCRIBE INJURIES	12. REFUSED TREATMENT YES ☐ NO ☐
#	13. TIME OF DEATH	14. PRONOUNCED BY	15. IDENTIFIED BY	

16. NEXT OF KIN	17. ADDRESS	18. RELATION	19. PHONE	20. NOTIFIED YES ☐ NO ☐

NOTE: FOR ADDITIONAL PERSONS USE ADDITIONAL PERSONS PAGE

SECTION 2 — SOLVABILITY FACTORS   PLACE (X) IF ANSWER IS YES

1. ( ) WAS A SUSPECT(S) ARRESTED?
   IF '1' IS YES AND NO OTHER SUSPECT(S) GO TO '6'
2. ( ) IS THERE A POSSIBLE SUSPECT(S)?
3. ( ) CAN A SUSPECT(S) BE NAMED?
4. ( ) CAN A SUSPECT(S) BE LOCATED?
5. ( ) CAN A SUSPECT(S) BE DESCRIBED?
6. ( ) IS THERE A WITNESS TO THE CRIME?
7. ( ) CAN THE SUSPECT(S) BE IDENTIFIED?
8. ( ) IS THERE A SUSPECT VEHICLE LICENSE NO?

9. ( ) IS THERE A SUSPECT VEHICLE DESCRIPTION?
10. ( ) IS THE STOLEN PROPERTY IDENTIFIABLE?
11. ( ) IS THERE A SIGNIFICANT M.O.?
12. ( ) IS THERE SIGNIFICANT PHYSICAL EVIDENCE?
13. ( ) HAS EVIDENCE BEEN SENT TO / OBTAINED BY IDENT?
14. ( ) HAS EVIDENCE BEEN SENT TO / OBTAINED BY CRIME LAB?
15. ( ) ARE THERE OTHER FACTORS THAT NECESSITATE A FOLLOW-UP INVESTIGATION?
16. ( ) IS THERE A SIGNIFICANT REASON TO BELIEVE THAT THE CRIME WILL BE SOLVED?

SECTION 3 — REPORTING OFFICER

1. NAME	2. RANK PIN	TEAM/SQ	3. ACCOMPANIED BY	4. RANK PIN
				DATE: YY / MM / DD

SECTION 4 — FOLLOW UP INVESTIGATION

1. CASE ASSIGNED TO	2. CASE ASSIGNED BY	3. DATE ASSIGNED	4. B.F. DATE

COPIES TO | 2 | 3 | 4 | 5 | 6 | 7 | 8 | 9

QUALITY CONTROL   DATA ENTRY   CASE REPORTS   RECORDS

Vancouver Police Department Investigation Report. An example of a Canadian reporting form.
(Courtesy of Chief Constable W. T. Marshall.)

ARIZONA DEPARTMENT OF PUBLIC SAFETY
CRIMINAL SUPPLEMENT TO TRAFFIC
ACCIDENT INVESTIGATION

1. DR. NO.

2. DATE & TIME OCCURRED	3. LOCATION OF OCCURRENCE	4. TYPE OF OFFENSE/INCIDENT	5. COUNTY

6.   DUI ☐   HIT & RUN ☐   AGGRAVATED ASSAULT ☐   ENDANGERMENT ☐   HOMICIDE ☐   **7. B A**

SUSPECT

8. NAME			9. ADDRESS					
10. BUSINESS ADDRESS		11. OCCUPATION	12. SEX	13. RACE	14. WGT.	15. HGT.	16. EYES	17. HAIR
18. SOCIAL SECURITY NUMBER	19. DRIVERS LICENSE NUMBER	20. PLACE OF BIRTH				21. DATE OF BIRTH		
22. HOME PHONE	23. BUSINESS PHONE	24. ALIAS, MARKS SCARS, TATOOS, ETC.						
25. LOCATION OF ARREST		26. DATE AND TIME OF ARREST		27. LOC. BOOKED OR REF.		28. CITATION NO.(S)		

VEHICLE

29. SUSPECT	30. COLOR	31. YEAR	32. MAKE	33. BODY STY.	34. LIC. NO.	35. STATE	36. OTHER ID.	37. VEHICLE DISPOSITION
38. VICTIM	39. COLOR	40. YEAR	41. MAKE	42. BODY STY.	43. LIC. NO.	44. STATE	45. OTHER DI.	46. VEHICLE DISPOSITION

VICTIM

47. NAME			48. ADDRESS					
49. BUSINESS ADDRESS		50. OCCUPATION	51. SEX	52. RACE	53. WGT.	54. HGT.	55. EYES	56. HAIR
57. SOCIAL SECURITY NUMBER	58. DRIVERS LICENSE NUMBER	59. PLACE OF BIRTH				60. DATE OF BIRTH		
61. OTHER				62. HOME PHONE		63. BUSINESS PHONE		

64. LIST ALL OTHER SUSPECTS/WITNESSES/INVESTIGATIVE LEADS/EVIDENCE

65.	66. OFFICER(S)		67. REVIEWED BY:
☐ PENDING		I.D. DISTRICT	
☐ CLOSED BY ARREST			68. DATE & TIME TYPED
☐ CLOSED, OTHER			69. CLERK NO.

DISTRIBUTION: WHITE: DEPT. RECORDS; YELLOW: PROSECUTOR; PINK: WORK COPY   802-04059 10/91

Arizona Department of Public Safety Traffic Accident Report. An example of a large agency's reporting form. *(Courtesy of Director F. J. "Rick" Ayars and Officer F. A. Stewart.)*

tem of storage, retrieval, and analysis, any law enforcement agency can be overwhelmed by a sea of paper.

Computers and Arrest Records

If paperwork can be seen as the mother's milk of bureaucracies, the Garden City, New York, Police Department is in the process of weaning itself, using a computer software program to reduce the time and tedium involved in arrest-related paperwork.

The JetForm software used by the department to process arrest paperwork is one of the agency's latest applications of computer technology, reports the April edition of *PC Publishing* magazine, and has cut from 4 hours to 40 minutes the time spent processing the myriad of forms that arrests generate.

Officer Al Perez, who has been in charge of the department's computerization effort since 1987, pointed out that JetForm can be used for a variety of tasks, including designing new forms when needed.

"We are doing most of our arrest forms, pedigree information sheets, vehicle accident reports, court information manuscripts, and the like in the program," said Perez. The JetForm program is compatible with the agency's PC-clone microcomputers, as well as the on-line printers in use by the agency, added Perez.

But the JetForm program is used most to process arrests, which require filling out local, state, and federal forms with pertinent data. Much of the data is redundant, but JetForm saves time by inserting repetitive items in the appropriate spaces of all of the various forms.

"Using the program greatly reduced the amount of time required to process an arrest. That's a welcome benefit," Perez said, noting that it saves overtime costs and hastens the return of the officers to patrol duties.

JetForm has features that allow the transfer and capture of information from one field to another—a capability that Perez said is "very handy."

"Scanning a form, tracing it out and using it as a template has worked out well, too," he added.

Perez said the 44-officer department will soon have its computer capabilities linked into a local-area network, and there are plans to acquire mobile data terminals, or laptops, for police cruisers. The terminals will be connected to a radio frequency and the local-area network at headquarters.

"Officers in the vehicles will be able to transmit information back to the department instantly, and that should boost the speed at which forms are processed," Perez explained.

The department's computerization program has streamlined the way paperwork is processed, Perez noted. "We produce anywhere from 6 to 100 forms daily. I could not imagine going back and doing things the old way."[4]

The preceding article indicates how computerization of certain records can save the department an immense amount of time.

Some departments began to utilize computers in certain sections of their records divisions in the early 1970s. Even if those areas were modernized within the last 10 years, their status should be reviewed with technical experts to ensure that recent advances have not made them obsolete.[5]

There are several areas of internal administration within a police department that can be computer enhanced with very little effort or expense.[6]

Training Records Individual officer training records are maintained by the department. These records may be entered into a computer and updated with very little effort. Many states require periodic training for all officers or advanced training for officers when a certain number of years has elapsed after their initial training. Computerized training records offer the department the ability to track the level and amount of training administered to each officer.

Personnel Personnel records, like training records, require a large amount of time to maintain and update. By placing these records in a computer, the department can quickly update and cross-reference them to other files, such as training records.

Scheduling of Personnel This used to be a cumbersome task that had to be redone every time a change was made. Computers allow a department to insert personnel changes and modify scheduled hours with a minimum of effort. Numerous factors that go into scheduling a 24-hour-a-day patrol can be entered into a computer to assist in determining the schedule.

Community Relations This area is gaining more importance in police work. A computer may assist the department by updating speaking schedules and maintaining lists of community associations and citizens who work with the department in solving community issues.

Vehicle Maintenance The ability to track maintenance schedules and repair costs is becoming more and more important in this era of tightening municipal and federal budgets. Tracking routine vehicle maintenance schedules and identifying the cost of upkeep is simplified with readily available software. Computerized systems allow immediate costing out of vehicle maintenance.

Purchasing The ability to keep track of items purchased by the department is closely related to the next area—budgeting. Purchasing and inventory control of such items as agency-supplied uniforms, paper, pencils, and so forth is a task requiring attention to detail and subject to multiple mistakes in accounting. Computers provide a method to update constantly changing inventories and cross-check figures.

Budgeting This is becoming a most critical area for every law enforcement agency. The need to project expenses (and in some cases revenues) accurately is an ideal requirement for software spreadsheet programs. Even if the department relies on the city finance or treasury department for final figures, many administrators feel the need to have their own in-house method. A typical spreadsheet program will cost $100 to $500 and is well worth the investment.

Payroll Closely related to budgeting is preparation of the departmental payroll. In many departments, this service is carried out by a centralized office outside the agency. Typically, the finance or treasury department will prepare payrolls. Similar to the use and preparation of budgets, some departments may desire to track payroll records to include sick time used, vacation taken, and other information that typically appears only on paystubs but which may be of interest to administrators.

A computerized records system standing by itself does not automatically ensure a more efficient records division. Computers will not think for humans. They process information that has been placed in the software program. Therefore, it is absolutely necessary that an effective records processing system be utilized in addition to putting information into computers. There are many variations concerning records processing within a police department. No matter what form or name they take, these records processing systems should include the ability to cross-reference all criminal activities. Cross-referencing or indexing criminal records requires that certain key information be indexed with other information so that anyone searching the database will be supplied with all other pertinent facts.

All crime indexing should include the following information:

1. The full name of the victim or complaining party.
2. The full name of the person arrested or suspected of committing the offense.
3. The name of the officer who took the offense report.
4. The name of the investigating officer.
5. The full names of all witnesses.
6. The classification of the crime.

Cross-indexing of crimes is critical to properly utilizing the *modus operandi concept.* Briefly stated, modus operandi is the method of operation. Certain people commit similar crimes using the same method each time. This leaves a "fingerprint" which assists the department in determining how many crimes have been committed by the same person, and in some instances may lead to the capture of the criminal. For example, a pattern or method of operation may be established showing that a rapist attacks young women and wears a stocking mask during the assault. Additionally, he may utter the same words to each victim at the same time during the rape. This becomes his MO. Even though some of the victims cannot identify his face, this MO may be sufficient for arrest and conviction of all the rapes he committed using that method.

Whenever the department cross-indexes crimes according to modus operandi, the method of operation should be further divided into the following areas:

1. Location—where the crime was committed.
2. Person or property attacked.
3. Time of the attack.
4. How the attack was carried out.
5. Method of attack.
6. Object of the attack.
7. Any special characteristics.

Every crime should be indexed. Once the information is input, the computer can analyze the data and produce variations that may assist in the capture of the offender.

Report processing is more than simply filling out forms in the correct manner. It involves indexing the information and utilizing computers to assist in the detection of criminal activity.

CONFIDENTIALITY OF RECORDS

The final aspect of law enforcement records that should be examined is the issue of confidentiality of police records. Many states have freedom-of-information laws that require all public records to be open for inspection by members of the public. Most of these statutes, however, set forth certain exceptions. Police records have traditionally been exempt from disclosure. The reasons for this exemption are obvious. If anyone could view investigative files, ongoing criminal investigations might be compromised.

Another area that causes friction between law enforcement officers and the media concerns the confidentiality of information regarding juveniles accused of committing crimes. Juvenile proceedings, as well as all the facts surrounding the case, are confidential. This protection is established by various state statutes. The rationale behind keeping juveniles' names and criminal acts confidential is that publicizing these incidents could stigmatize the juveniles and possibly prevent rehabilitation. This area continues to be debated and will undoubtedly continue to generate high public emotion.

The confidentiality of records is an area of high emotion when the department deals with members of the media. The media will argue that the public has a right to know, and that the police department does not have the right to refuse to release information, especially if the case has been referred to the district attorney for the filing of criminal charges.

Confidentiality and Police Informants

Informants expose crimes that otherwise may go undetected. When properly used and controlled, they provide information that improves police efficiency, assists in the apprehension and prosecution of criminals, and sometimes even prevents crimes from taking place.

However, to use informants effectively, agencies must establish and maintain strict, written departmental policies on handling informants. Even when operating under tight controls, informants can quickly go bad or become unreliable. When they do, they create significant legal and public relations problems.

Only those with a need to know should be advised of an informant's identity. In practical terms, this means investigators and their alternates who work closely with the source. The squad supervisor or first-line manager should be encouraged to meet the informant, so that the source knows there are people in authority who support the program, and so that the manager has a general "feel" for the informant. The person who controls the informant file room must also know an informant's identity in order to handle the filing and other paperwork. These employees should be the only people who routinely handle informant information and who need to know the informant's identity.

To ensure secrecy, informants should be assigned code numbers and code names. These take the place of the source's real name on all documents and reports, and also in personal conversations. Any information provided by the source must be documented and recorded using code numbers and code names.

The files created must be maintained in secure rooms and access to them must be strictly controlled by an employee specifically assigned to control access. Only the informant's handler or alternate handler and the immediate supervisor should be allowed to examine those files routinely. A daily record that lists everyone who enters the secure room should also be maintained. This control is not implemented to create a bureaucratic roadblock, but to protect sources by limiting the number of people who know their identities. Institutionally, it also reinforces the importance of protecting informants' identities.

Source: Adapted from Harry A. Mount, Jr., "Criminal Informants, An Administrator's Dream or Nightmare," *FBI Law Enforcement Bulletin* (Dec. 1990): 12.

The department may be concerned that releasing the results of an investigation prior to a conviction may influence members of the public and impact the prosecutor's ability to find an impartial jury. For the most part, this area of the law is controlled by statutes that govern the withholding of information and set forth specific guidelines for the release of police department files.

SUMMARY

Basic law enforcement records may vary from jurisdiction to jurisdiction, but the principles behind their utilization will remain the same. There are two basic types of reports—operational and administrative. Each serves a vital purpose, and to neglect one in favor of the other is to destroy the effectiveness of any records division—and ultimately the operational capability of the agency.

Law enforcement, by its very nature, involves access to or use of confidential information. Many times this information is recorded in reports. This may cause a conflict with members of the media who would like access to those records. However, criminal justice professionals must keep those records confidential if they are to retain their credibility.

REVIEW QUESTIONS

1. What is the most important aspect of a police records system?

2. Should law enforcement agencies use computers and not maintain any paper records? Why? Why not? Read the chapter dealing with management information systems and determine if that changes your mind.

3. This chapter contains examples of reports from a small, a large, and an international law enforcement agency. What are the differences in the forms? What are the similarities?

4. List some reasons why police records should remain confidential even after the case has been sent to the prosecuting attorney.

BETTER WRITING DRILLS

Problems with Verbs

Verbs cause more problems than any other part of speech because of the far greater number of forms they can take. Following are some of the common problems that appear in crime reports.

Number Verbs must agree with the subject in number. As a general rule, if the subject refers to a group as a whole, it is *singular.* If the subject refers to the individual members, it is *plural.*

The majority was overruled.
The government was formed.
The audience rose to their feet.

If a verb relates to two or more nouns connected by a *coordinate conjunction,* the following rules apply:

1. If it agrees with them conjointly, it takes a plural.

   The officer and her dog were reunited.
   Both the pilot and the copilot were at the controls of the airplane.

2. If the verb agrees with the nouns separately, it takes the number of the noun that stands next to it.

   Neither the suspect nor the victims were located.
   Neither the victims nor the suspect was located.

3. If the verb agrees with one noun and not the other, it takes the number of the one in the affirmative.

   The suspects and not the victim are responsible.
   The suspect and not the victims is responsible.

Certain pronouns take singular verbs, for example, *anybody, everybody, everyone, nobody, somebody, each, either, no one,* and *someone.*

When singular and plural subjects are joined by constructions (like both . . . and, either . . . or, not only . . . but), the verb takes on the number of the subject closest to it.

   Neither the victim nor the suspects were aware of the fire.
   Neither the victims nor the suspect was aware of the fire.

A clause or phrase that comes between the subject and the verb should not affect the number of the verb.

   The initial training, not to mention follow-up training, was substantial.

Voices In an earlier chapter, we discussed use of the active and passive voice. As noted earlier, the *active voice* focuses attention on the doer and the *passive voice* focuses on what has been done. Your writing will be more forceful and concise if the active voice is used.

   Active: Earthquakes have damaged parts of California.
   Passive: Parts of the state have been damaged by earthquakes.

Mood Verbs, like people, have various moods. The mood of a verb enables the verb to express attitudes and intentions.

1. The *indicative* mood is used in most statements and questions. This is the most common mood. It states a fact or asks a question.

   The victim left no writings.

2. The *imperative* mood is used in commands or requests.

   Read the words of Marvin Wolfgang.

3. The *subjunctive* mood is used when expressing a conditional statement that is dubious, doubtful, or contrary to known facts.

   If the officer were to read the statements, she would find that the facts are different.

PRACTICAL APPLICATIONS

1. Examine how you retain your personal records. Are they organized so that a stranger could find a specific item? How would you change your record-keeping system based on your reading of this chapter?

2. Ask to review your college record. Inquire how it is maintained and updated. In your opinion, is this the most effective record-keeping system? What changes would you recommend?

3. Ask another student to describe the appearance of another instructor at your university or college. Write a description of the instructor; however, do not write down the instructor's name, and ask another student to identify the instructor on the basis of your written report.

4. In each of the rows below, circle the correctly spelled word:

tranfer	trensfer	transfer	tranfere
translator	tranlator	translater	transletor
transfered	tranferred	transfar	transferred
treasuror	traesuror	treasurer	traesurror
trafficking	traficking	trafick	trafick
wounded	wounde	wuonde	woundlie
wather	waether	wheathar	whether
wittness	witness	wetiness	witeness
wristly	wristely	wriste	wrist
widthe	width	wedth	widthi

5. Rewrite the following sentences as needed:

   a. The datum were correct.

b. Me and Tom was both correct.

_____

c. The accident was observed by me and my partner.

_____

d. The mob of looters were working in new city.

_____

e. An officer never forgets their first arrest.

_____

6. Define and explain the following words or terms:
   a. law enforcement records system

   _____

   b. functions of record division

   _____

   c. cross-indexing of crimes

   _____

   d. confidentiality of records

   _____

   e. active voice

   _____

7. The following paragraph was taken from an actual police report. Make it a better paragraph.

   At which time, this officer dismounted from his police unit and upon arrival observed a male subject driving a blue car that appeared to be an old model Ford. The subject was hiding his face and refused to dismount from the vehicle. This officer order the subject to get out of the vehicle. The subject acted like he did not hear this officer. I then approached the subject car and noted that the individual had a gun in his hand. This officer immediately called for backup and when the car was surrounded by other police officers the subject threw out his weapon which on furhter examination revealed that the suspected weapon was a toy pistol.

   _____

   _____

   _____

   _____

WORDS TO KNOW

authentic	demonstration
authoritative	effective
auxiliary	familiar
benefited	imminent
breadth	maintain
calendar	obstacle
cashier	preferable
classification	report
convenience	television
cylinder	tournament

ENDNOTES

1. See, for example, O. W. Wilson's classic article, "Records and Their Installation" (Washington, D.C.: International City Management Association), 73–137.

2. Dennis George, "Computer-Assisted Report Entry: Toward a Paperless Police Department," *The Police Chief* (Mar. 1990): 46.

3. For an excellent discussion of an effective system, see George J. Schmidt, "Computer System Improves Law Enforcement Operation," *The Police Chief* (Dec. 1994): 20.

4. Reprinted from *Law Enforcement News* 16, no. 311 (Mar. 31, 1990): 7.

5. See "Information at Your Fingertips," *Law and Order* (Feb. 1995): 54

6. See "Focus on Communications," a special issue dealing with computers, *Law and Order* (Feb. 1995).

9

Management Information Systems

KEY TERMS

Computer-aided dispatch (CAD)—A computerized system that responds to requests for information with detailed information concerning the facts necessary for a patrol officer to act.

Computer system—A collection of components that interact to achieve some goal.

Crime analysis—Identification, description, and dissemination of information concerning crime patterns and problems.

Incident-based reporting (IBR)—Agencies submit designated characteristics and information pertaining to each prescribed crime or arrest incident, rather than submitting aggregate monthly statistics.

Intelligence analysis—The collection, analysis, and dissemination of information concerning organized crime.

Management information system—Provides past, present, and projected information about the law enforcement agency and its operating environment.

National Crime Information Center (NCIC)—A computerized records system containing information regarding outstanding warrants, inventories of stolen property, criminal histories, and other information that may assist law enforcement agencies in investigating cases.

Operations analysis—The interpretation of problems relating to the operations of the law enforcement agency.

Procedures—Written instructions for use and operation of the computer system.

Program—A specific set of electronic instructions that tells the computer to accomplish a list of tasks.

INTRODUCTION TO COMPUTER SYSTEMS

Most students in college or university have either used or, at the very least, been exposed to computers. Many consider themselves experts and some have become hackers. The use of computers has permeated our society, from the use of campus automated tellers to withdraw cash from a bank account to the preparation of grade lists at the end of the semester.

For many students and professionals, using software programs to type term papers, draft spreadsheets, and establish databases is a common, everyday experience. However, there are many college graduates and professionals who, while they have been exposed to computers and draw on their convenience, have never gained a solid understanding of computer systems. A study by Microsoft indicates that while many workers use computers at their places of employment, they are still uncomfortable with computers and do not use them in their homes.

A computer system is a collection of components that interact to achieve some goal.[1] This definition makes it clear that a system is more all inclusive than a simple computer. The following sections explain the different parts of a computer system and how those components interact.

The Components of a Computer System

Prior to examining specific police information systems, it is necessary to review some basic principles. These principles apply to police computer systems whether they are utilized at a local, state, or national level.

The five components of a basic law enforcement computer system are (1) hardware, (2) programs or software, (3) data, (4) procedures, and (5) personnel. Failure to include or properly utilize any of these components will lead to an inefficient use of already scarce resources.

Hardware This component is the one most people are familiar with, since they can see it. It is the physical machine we see, touch, and use. The hardware component is made up of four sections: (1) input equipment, (2) processing equipment, (3) output equipment, and (4) storage equipment.

The *input equipment* is used to send information into the computer. Common input devices are the *keyboard* and *mouse.*

The *processing equipment* does the actual computing once it receives the information or data from the input device. Most processing equipment is located inside the computer. The name associated with processing equipment is *central processing unit (CPU).*

The third section of hardware is the *output equipment.* Output equipment transfers data from the CPU to an output device so it can be used or read by the computer user. This is typified by *viewing monitors* and *printers.*

The last section of the hardware component is the *storage equipment.* The computer's brain, or CPU, has a limited capacity to retain information; therefore, it is necessary to store this data in a storage device. Storage devices include *tape, hard disks,* or *diskettes.*

Programs or Software Once a computer is constructed, it has the ability to accomplish many tasks. However, unless it is given directions, it is simply an expensive office machine. A *program* is a specific set of electronic instructions that tells the computer to accomplish a list of tasks. Word processing software packages such as Microsoft Word or WordPerfect are computer programs. Lotus 1-2-3 is a *spreadsheet application,* another example of a computer program. Programs can be written or created in a number of *computer languages.* Some of the more common or well-known languages are PASCAL, BASIC, and COBOL. There are two basic categories of programs: systems programs and application programs. *Systems programs* control the computer. They cause it to start and stop assignments, copy data from one location to another, and perform other necessary but generic tasks. An example of a systems program would be DOS (disk operating system). Most systems programs are included in the basic price of the computer system. *Application programs* are specifically created for certain tasks. An example of an application program would be software that performs payroll functions. Most application programs must either be specifically created to fill a perceived need or purchased separately for the computer system.

Data The third component of a law enforcement computer system is *data.* Before any need can be addressed, all pertinent facts must be gathered. For example, before making any logical law enforcement response to a rising burglary rate, it is necessary to gather all the critical facts surrounding the burglaries, including whether there is any pattern to the crimes. This is a critical area for computer systems because all data must be placed in the computer before it can be analyzed. It is placed in the computer by an input device.

There is a difference between data and information. Data are recorded facts or figures. Information is knowledge that is derived from data. For example, a list of arrests made during the last month is data, while a summary of arrests by each officer, together with the names of the top three officers who made the most burglary arrests, would be information derived from the arrest data.

Computer data may be broken down into four areas: (1) input data that is read into the computer for processing, (2) processing data inside the CPU, (3) output data that is the result of the analysis, and (4) storage data. The last is data that is stored for future use on a tape, hard disk, or diskette.

Procedures *Procedures* are written instructions for use and operation of the computer system. Anyone purchasing a new computer usually receives operating instructions on how to set up the computer. Additionally, many software programs come with a manual explaining how to install and use the program. The number of classes offered by colleges and universities, as well as in private industry, on how to run certain software programs such as WordPerfect attests to the need for clear, concise, and understandable procedures.

Personnel The final component of a computer system is the people who are involved. There are *system development personnel* who design computer systems, *operational personnel* who operate the system, and *users* who interact with the system. Users provide data for consumption by the computer and use the computer-generated information to carry out their assignments.

Computers and the FBI

The FBI Laboratory in Washington, D.C., is using computers in almost every phase of its operations. Our Serology Unit handles over 40,000 samples each year. The high number of samples analyzed makes a clerical nightmare of creating, manipulating, maintaining, disseminating, and storing a huge volume of data. However, those problems are being solved through the use of automation. The evidence examiners place their work orders into the computer, from which the technicians receive those work orders automatically.

Upon completion of the necessary tests, results are entered into the computer by the technicians for review by the evidence examiners. The results can be compared automatically against known standards and population statistics.

- A computer-based system to aid in the examination of firearms evidence is being developed at the Forensic Science Research and Training Center at the FBI Academy in Quantico, Virginia.

- Computers have become an integral part of the modern forensic library. An essential aspect of information services is searching the available literature. An efficient way to do this is by searching online databases. The Forensic Science Information Resource System (FSIRS) utilizes the Dialog Information Retrieval Service. Dialog currently has more than 300 online bibliographic, statistical, and full text databases with excellent multidisciplinary coverage.

- Through the sustained use of computers and their expanding capabilities, law enforcement will continue to grow as a profession in the future.

Computers and computer systems continue to become faster, smaller, and capable of holding more data. Additionally, as technology expands the capabilities of computers, it will become more critical for law enforcement professionals to stay abreast of the changes so as to provide up-to-date advice to their departments.

Management Information Systems

To fully understand management information systems, it is necessary to compare them with other computer applications. There are two other computer systems that are of interest to law enforcement professionals: *operations information systems* and *command and control systems.* Although some authorities consider these systems separate and distinct from management information systems, they all are based on the same principles.[2] No matter what name is attached to the system—operational, command, or management—the purpose of these systems is to provide the administrator with critical information that is distilled from more general data.

Operations information systems provide information to those officers who are actively engaged in preserving the public peace. This information is normally utilized by the patrol officer or detective involved in the day-to-day activities of law enforcement on the street. The officers often need information rapidly and need assurance that it is accurate. Operational information might include whether a person is wanted, the arrest record of a suspect, the status of a case, and so forth. Many times this information is needed to assist the officer in making a decision on what course of action to take. Later in this chapter, automated records and communications systems will be examined. These systems assist the individual officer and the agency by providing a means to transmit operational information in a rapid manner.

Command and control systems provide information to top-level management, allowing them to make informed decisions. These systems allow watch officers to monitor a critical situation and provide a method of coordinating tactical services when necessary. For example, if a group of people is being held hostage, command and control information systems allow coordination between police, fire, and other agencies involved.

Operations information systems and command and control systems are important in the overall operation of a law enforcement agency. However, the most critical computer system is the *management information system (MIS).* A management information system provides past, present, and projected information about the law enforcement agency and its operating environment.

A management information system may provide services in three ways: (1) providing regular recurring reports, (2) producing exception reports, and (3) providing information to ad hoc inquiries. The last category is also known as *decision reports.* In the first group of services are *regular recurring reports,* which might include the daily or monthly reports issued in a local law enforcement agency. The *exception reports* might include statistics that illustrate exceptional or unusual conditions, such as an increase in the number of officer-involved accidents. The third category of MIS services is decision reports. These reports allow top-level management of the law enforcement agency to improve the quality of any particular decision by providing all the necessary information on which the decision may be based. Since major decisions do not occur on a regular basis, this service is classified as an ad hoc inquiry.

The amount of information any law enforcement manager can assimilate is limited. Granted, there are exceptional leaders in the police community who retain an incredible amount of detail; however, the typical law enforcement administrator is unable to recall all the details of every facet of the department's daily operation. To assist law enforcement supervisory personnel in carrying out their assignments, management information services provide the ability to consolidate vast amounts of information into certain categories.

The two primary techniques of consolidating information are aggregation and generalization. *Aggregation* of data occurs when like data are combined across categories. For example, daily arrest data can be aggregated into monthly reports that show the total number of arrests for the month. This aggregation can take several forms. One form might list the total number of arrests for rape in the city, while another might list arrests for rape in a particular patrol district. *Generalization* of data combines unlike objects but ignores their differences. For example, the administrator may want to divide the division into two classes: inexperienced and experienced officers. The administrator may decide that any officer with less than one year on the force will be grouped into the inexperienced category, and all other officers will be classed as experienced. Clearly, all officers with more than one year with the department have differing amounts of experience, but for the purposes of generalization that fact is disregarded.

This section has discussed certain basic details that would apply to almost any computer system. The following sections build on this general knowledge and apply it to management information systems in law enforcement.

MANAGEMENT INFORMATION SYSTEMS AND LAW ENFORCEMENT

Management information systems have provided law enforcement with a valuable tool in the fight against crime. They allow police departments to analyze a tremendous amount of information in a relatively short period of time. The analysis of information takes several forms, as discussed in the next section.

Analysis of Police Information

Data received by the police does not automatically translate itself into information that will lead to an arrest. All data must be analyzed and applied. Law enforcement agencies must undertake several different types of information analysis. *Crime analysis, operations analysis,* and *intelligence analysis* are three of the more common types of analysis undertaken by police departments.

Crime Analysis The myth of Sherlock Holmes belongs in books or movies and not in a modern law enforcement agency. Very few police officers are able to solve crimes by simply viewing the scene of an offense and coming to a conclusion about who committed the crime and why.

Crime analysis involves answering questions such as these: Who committed the crime?, Why did it occur?, How was it accomplished?, and so on. The basic goal of crime analysis is to "identify, describe, and disseminate information concerning crime patterns and problems."[3] This analysis is aimed at discovering patterns or trends. Similar to analyzing an offender's modus operandi, crime analysis attempts to predict future occurrences. The analysis of a series of burglaries may establish a pattern of break-ins that are localized within a neighborhood. This knowledge might allow the department to allocate its resources in such a manner as to prevent further crimes or apprehend the criminal responsible for the burglaries.

Once the analysis is completed, the information is disseminated to patrol officers and detectives. This usually occurs during briefings or by distributing printouts at roll call.[4]

Crime analysis involves sifting through data for specific items of information and then collating that knowledge into usable form. Traditionally, crime analysis has been done manually. For instance, crimes were plotted on a city map when detectives assigned to the burglary division attempted to gain an overview of those offenses. The detectives went through all related crime reports, obtained the addresses of victims or locations where the crimes occurred, noted the date, time, and any other pertinent information, and then transferred that information to a city map with pins to mark the locations.

Modern police agencies utilize computers to conduct crime analysis. While the scenario described in the preceding paragraph might have taken hours to accomplish manually, a computer can provide that information literally in seconds. This information will be displayed on the computer terminal or printed in either a preestablished format or in any form the officers desire. Depending on the sophistication of the computer system and software program, some computerized crime analysis outputs may even superimpose the locations on a copy of a city map.

Crime analysis is an effective law enforcement tool that is enhanced by the use of computers. To be successful, however, crime analysis must be integrated into the flow of other information that is available to the police administrator.

Operations Analysis Operations analysis is the interpretation of problems relating to the operations of the law enforcement agency. It does not deal with crimes or other public protection issues. The operation of a police department provides numerous opportunities for gathering and analyzing information. The analysis of information may relate to short-term problems or provide guidelines for long-range planning. All of these areas involve the use of information concerning the administration of the department.

Long-range or strategic planning involves setting goals for projects five or more years in the future. Depending on the approach utilized, the chief of police may set the department's long-range goals, or the city manager may establish strategic goals and then require the chief to respond from a law enforcement position. In either situation, it is necessary to take known facts and trends and project them into the future to answer many of the issues raised in long-range or strategic planning. Such planning can be done with greater accuracy and speed using a computer system.

The most common form of immediate operational analysis deals with the allocation and deployment of patrol officers. The patrol division usually involves the greatest portion of a law enforcement agency's resources and is its most complex area from an administrative perspective.

The allocation of resources for patrol activities involves consideration of the following issues:

1. Developing or modifying patrol beats.
2. Adopting procedures for the dispatch and deployment of patrol assets.
3. Scheduling personnel to ensure coverage of patrol beats on a 24-hour basis, if necessary.
4. Determining the number of units on each patrol beat based on law enforcement needs.[5]

To make these decisions, operational data must be collected and analyzed. These data include the number of calls for service, the nature of the calls, response time to Priority 1 calls for service (generally life-threatening events), and the activity of each patrol officer. This would be the minimum information necessary to analyze the needs of the patrol division. Additionally, any information concerning trends in crimes or unusual criminal activity should be included in any operational analysis. This information allows the patrol supervisor to make an informed decision regarding which area of the municipality requires the largest number of officers on a given patrol beat at any particular time.

This analysis was traditionally carried out manually. However, a computer-based operational analysis provides speed and flexibility. The police administrator can review various options in a matter of minutes simply by changing some variables and requesting a new analysis. Crime analysis and operational analysis encompass most of the day-to-day issues that face a law enforcement agency. However, there is one additional form of analysis, *intelligence analysis,* that must be discussed when one considers the review of police information.

Intelligence Analysis Intelligence analysis involves the collection, analysis, and dissemination of information concerning organized crime. This is one of the most sensitive activities of any law enforcement agency. The sources of criminal intelligence are widespread and, in many instances, sensitive. They include information received from private citizens, confidential reliable informants, undercover agents, and other law enforcement agencies.

The need to keep this information confidential and separate from other police records is obvious. Release of the sources of some of this information might compromise an undercover operation or, worse yet, endanger an agent or source.

Because so many sources are providing different types of information, there is a need to sort through them, analyze the contents, and disseminate the information to the proper persons. Although much of this information may not solve a crime, it can provide leads that result in the arrest and conviction of organized crime figures. Sometimes, simply knowing who is involved with what group is important.

Information obtained from intelligence files is particularly helpful when dealing with street gangs, narcotics dealers, and terrorists. The problem occurs in sorting through all the details that find their way into the intelligence files. Any law enforcement agency utilizing intelligence records should adopt minimum standards regarding their collection, use, and dissemination.[6]

Computers assist the intelligence section commander in processing the large amount of information that may be available to the department. This information may assist other departmental divisions in carrying out their missions.

Communication Systems

Another aspect of police records is the ability to transfer information from the field to headquarters and vice versa. Just as law enforcement has progressed from manually searching reports, so has it improved in the area of transmitting information.[7] Without the ability to communicate information obtained from police files, the officer in the field is working under a tremendous handicap that may place that officer or others in danger.

Computer-Aided Dispatch (CAD) The development of computer-aided dispatch has improved the ability of departments to transmit information to officers in the field and has allowed them to improve response time by more effectively assigning patrol officers on a beat. CAD is a computerized system that responds to requests for information with detailed information concerning the facts necessary for the patrol officer to act. Depending on the software package used by the department, the CAD system may verify addresses, recommend the safest access route, inform the dispatcher which patrol unit is closest to the address, and inform the officer of any dangerous situation, such as the possibility that a known felon is residing at the premise.

The computer-aided dispatch system will record the time and nature of all calls for service, provide a real-time monitoring system of patrol vehicle status and an update of incidents, and allow supervisors to monitor the daily activity of the patrol division.

Initially, CADs were connected to mobile digital terminals (MDTs) located in the patrol vehicle.[8] These MDTs were rather limited, but they could access some databases and send short messages. In technologically advanced departments, MDTs are being replaced with mobile communications terminals (MCTs). These terminals allow the officer to communicate with the department's records division without tying up a dispatcher. MCTs range from the very simple single-item query to the complex computer-enhanced terminal. While this type of communication may seem more appropriate for Dick Tracy, these devices have been available since the early 1980s.

In a classic analysis of police communication programs, Colton *et al.* listed the following features of mobile communications systems[9]:

1. Assures the operator that all necessary information is obtained from the complainant.
2. Verifies the location and address.
3. Determines the patrol beat or district where the incident is located.
4. Assigns priorities to calls.
5. Reports on any previous calls from the location.
6. Routes calls to the appropriate dispatchers.
7. Recommends assignment of patrol vehicles to respond to calls based on location of the call and status of the patrol units.
8. Records time of calls, time of arrival by patrol units, and time cleared from the scene.
9. Tracks status of patrol units and incidents.

Computer-aided dispatch is an efficient form of communication that allows officers to gain access to police records quickly.

E-Mail E-mail, or electronic mail, has become the new telephone system within public agencies. Many larger law enforcement departments have adopted E-mail to communicate internally as well as externally. E-mail uses a modem and software to allow an officer to type a message into a computer and send it electronically to another computer within the department, the city, or even another country.

E-mail offers officers the ability to send a message to one or more persons with a word processing or other type of file attached for their review. Those individuals are then able to edit and return that file to the sender. This allows worldwide communication and instantaneous feedback to the author of the message.

E-mail offers several advantages over the telephone: it can be sent even if no one is there to receive it, it allows a written record to be maintained, and once received it can be added to or modified and forwarded to other parties. Many users can log on from their home computers and read and send messages without having to go to the office.

Facsimile (Fax) Machines Fax machines have become so common in law enforcement agencies that most supervisors include their fax numbers on their business cards. These machines allow officers to send pictures, text, and anything else that can be copied to any place where there is another fax machine and a telephone line. They have become as indispensable as photocopiers.

The Information Superhighway or Internet The terms *Information Superhighway* and *Internet* describe a massive worldwide network of computers. The word Internet actually means a network of computers. The Internet is composed of thousands of smaller regional computer networks.

The *World Wide Web* is the most popular facility, and the most powerful system, on the Internet. It looks like a color magazine containing pictures, sound recordings, video clips, and text. Many programs allow a user to click on a key word and search other sources of data. All major operating systems include access programs that allow users to connect to the Internet. The Department of Justice and many other governmental agencies can be contacted via the Internet. It is therefore imperative that law enforcement officers have a basic understanding of the various sources of information contained on the Internet.

The 9-1-1 System Most citizens are familiar with the 9-1-1 telephone number. This system provides one number, 9-1-1, to contact a law enforcement agency in the event of an emergency, and has gained widespread acceptance from the public and police. What many citizens and some law enforcement personnel do not realize is that the 9-1-1 system is a form of computerized dispatching.

The computer process calls for assistance and, depending on the software program adopted by the jurisdiction, displays key information on a screen in front of the telephone operator/dispatcher. A basic 9-1-1 system provides a display of the number and address of the calling party, automatic routing to the appropriate jurisdiction, and supplementary support data consisting of the patrol beat, firebox locations, and ambulance zones.[10]

Some of the data in the 9-1-1 system will come from the police department's records division. This information would include the boundaries of the various patrol beats and other information that would be input to the 9-1-1 computer so the dispatcher can make the necessary decisions. The 9-1-1 system is a perfect example of computers, records, and humans working together to protect the public.

Automated Records

An automated records system allows a law enforcement agency to maintain a large amount of information in a database with the ability to retrieve selected items immediately. This system is linked to computer-aided dispatch programs that give the officer in the field access to criminal histories, wants and warrants, and other important information.

These systems may be very simple or extremely complex depending on the needs, finances, and goals of the department. Some of the more sophisticated systems offer the following options:

1. *Special warning messages.* This information might include background data on a person, such as "armed and dangerous."
2. *Verification of addresses.* This program verifies the address and location of a residence and lists the known occupants.
3. *AKA information.* This program lists alias or "also known as" names of individuals.

Access to this type of information allows law enforcement officers to make the necessary decisions in the field safely and immediately.[11] There is very little downtime waiting for information to be forwarded to the patrol officer. Automated records systems coupled with access to regional or national records systems provide up-to-the-minute information regarding suspects contacted by the officer.

National Incident-Based Reporting System (NIBRS)

The National Incident-Based Reporting System was developed by the FBI with the assistance of the International Association of Chiefs of Police (ICAP), the National Sheriffs Association (NSA), state-level Uniform Crime Reporting (UCR) programs, the National Alliance of State Drug Enforcement Agencies, the Drug Enforcement Administration, and various federal, state, and local criminal justice agencies.

In the Incident-Based Reporting (IBR) system, agencies submit designated characteristics and information pertaining to each prescribed crime or arrest incident, rather than aggregate monthly statistics. The NIBRS collects information on 22 broad crime categories and utilizes 52 data elements to collect and analyze information about these crimes. The data elements provide vital information about crime and its involvement with victims, offenders, property, arrestees, and so forth.

Collecting the proper data over a period of time can realize certain benefits in the way crime data are used. For example, NIBRS data can be used to show when and where crime occurs, what form it takes, and the characteristics of its victims and perpetrators, enabling a particular locale to institute more efficient patrol operations. The objective of NIBRS is not to require the collection of additional data by law enforcement participants but to better utilize the information that is already being collected in the ordinary course of business.[12]

NCIC and Regional Systems

The National Crime Information Center (NCIC) is a computerized records system maintained in Washington, D.C. NCIC contains information regarding outstanding warrants, inventories of stolen property, criminal histories, and other information that may assist law enforcement agencies in investigating cases. This national electronic information center was developed by the Federal Bureau of Investigation and is structured in such a manner that local law enforcement agencies have access to a national criminal information database in seconds.[13]

NCIC is administrated by the FBI with the cooperation of local, state, regional, and federal law enforcement agencies. The NCIC receives policy direction from the director of the FBI, who in turn relies on the NCIC Advisory Policy Board. This board is composed of a select group of top administrators from criminal justice agencies throughout the United States. The board recommends changes in procedures to update the NCIC system.

Currently 10 areas of data are contained in the NCIC: (1) Criminal Histories, (2) Missing Persons, (3) Wanted Persons, (4) Stolen Securities, (5) Stolen License Plates, (6) Recovered Guns, (7) Stolen Boats, (8) Stolen Articles, (9) Stolen and Felony Vehicles, and (10) Criminalistics Laboratory Information System. The NCIC provides a valuable nationwide source of information to law enforcement agencies that supplements regional systems.

The Uniform Crime Report's National Incident-Based Reporting System brings new capabilities to the FBI[14]. The Integrated Automated Fingerprint Identification System (IAFIS) increases the FBI's ability to maintain a current and effective fingerprint system.

When fully implemented, by using the NCIC-2000 system, patrol officers will be able to identify suspects simply by placing a suspect's finger on a fingerprint reader in the patrol car. A printer installed in the patrol vehicle will receive pictures of suspects, images of stolen goods, and composite drawings of unknown subjects.

The FBI has created the Criminal Justice Information Services (CJIS) division to support the criminal justice community. This division will provide state-of-the-art identification and information services. The CJIS will be able to respond to the changing technologies of the future.

Several states have computerized regional justice information centers. California and New York specifically have examples of statewide records systems that assist local law enforcement agencies in the performance of their mission by providing them with information.

Statewide Emergency Response Communications Systems

Some states have gone beyond regional justice information centers and have established a statewide emergency response communications system.

The state of Pennsylvania supports a statewide police emergency radio frequency. Using a multichannel radio programmed with each frequency used in a specific location, officers can monitor operational radio transmissions and then initiate an immediate response, while being able to communicate directly with the agency having jurisdictional responsibility for the incident.

The Pennsylvania State Police (PSP) purchased a 32–128 channel programmable mobile radio with the intent of expanding its own radio frequency resources. Then each communications specialist within the 15 troop areas statewide contacted all governmental agencies within their individual areas to request permission to program the PSP radio with the frequencies of those agencies. The response was overwhelming and included the neighboring states of Ohio, Delaware, and New York.

Currently, the state of Pennsylvania's Police Commission Division is responsible for managing 52 authorized radio programs used throughout the commonwealth by troopers. No longer must troopers wait for information to be relayed through another agency's dispatcher to a PSP dispatcher and then to them. Now, they simply monitor the original conversation and converse directly with the dispatcher of the agency having jurisdictional responsibility.

Source: Robert C. Hickes, "Pennsylvania's Interdepartmental Communications System," *FBI Law Enforcement Bulletin* (Sept. 1990): 18.

The regional systems typically contain arrest records, stolen vehicle listings, wants and warrants information, and detailed criminal histories. Regional systems operate in a manner very similar to the NCIC. Local agencies may send electronic inquiries to the system and it will respond in seconds with the requested information.

Information management systems vary from simple card files to massive computers that store large amounts of information. Increasing technology has allowed law enforcement agencies to increase the effectiveness of their operations by utilizing computers.

SUMMARY

Information management in law enforcement has expanded beyond the use of three-by-five cards and a simple one-minute briefing at roll call. The true professional must understand the operation of modern computer systems. This requires more than a knowledge of microcomputer word processing programs. Computers are constantly evolving and offering more alternatives to the law enforcement community.

The use of computers has enhanced law enforcement's ability to obtain information. With advanced computer-based systems, supervisors can observe the location and status of any patrol vehicle on a particular beat.

National and regional computerized information centers provide instantaneous transmission of information for use by the officer on the street. As crime becomes more sophisticated and fiscal pressures increase, law enforcement agencies will look toward computerization to save costs and enhance service to the public.

REVIEW QUESTIONS

1. Why are computers important to law enforcement agencies? Should agencies require every officer to be familiar with computers? Why? Why not?

2. Should agencies buy or lease computers? What are the advantages and disadvantages of each method?

3. Should we be collecting information in state and national databases on individuals? What about a person's right of privacy?

BETTER WRITING DRILLS

Sentences

Every sentence must have at least two parts, a *subject* (noun) and a *verb*. The *subject* names what you are talking about and the *verb* tells something about the action of the noun. One of the best ways to learn to write correct sentences is to read and pay attention to how others construct sentences. Research has established a high correlation between the person who reads a lot and the person who writes well.

Steps in writing better sentences include:

1. Writing in complete sentences; include both a subject and verb.

   Wrong: And began hitting the victim.

   Better: The suspect began hitting the victim.

2. Avoid the use of sentence fragments.

   Wrong: The officer chased the accused. And caught him.

   Better: The officer chased the accused and caught him.

3. Do not use run-on sentences. A run-on sentence is one which contains two or more complete sentences that are incorrectly joined together. The run-on sentence usually goes on too long without having any clear connection between its clauses and phrases. One method of preventing run-on sentences is to visualize their structure. The various sentence structures are as follows:

   - *Simple sentence.* A simple sentence contains one independent clause. *(The officer stopped the car.)*
   - *Complex sentence.* The complex sentence contains one and only one independent clause and one or more dependent clauses. *(The officer is the one who came early.)* The dependent clause may come first, in which case a

comma usually sets it off from the independent clause. *(While in the car, the officer used the radio.)*

- *Compound sentence.* A compound sentence contains two or more independent clauses but no dependent clauses or coordinating conjunctions.
- *Compound-complex sentence.* A compound-complex sentence contains at least two independent clauses and one dependent clause as a basic structure.

Long, legal sentences are frequently used by attorneys. Although they may be correct in form, it is risky for an officer to imitate "legalese." Another problem with run-on sentences is that confusion sometimes exists as to which subject goes with which verb. Often the use of a comma and a simple connecting word such as *but, and, or, nor,* or *so* will correct the run-on sentence. In some cases, it is correct to use a semicolon and no connecting word.

Wrong: The officer contacted the victim and he informed the victim that he had the property.

Better: The officer contacted the victim, and he informed the victim that he had the property.

- Often, combining several short sentences into a longer sentence will improve the clarity of the writing. *Note:* Unrelated ideas should not be combined into a single sentence.

Jerry is a college student. He is 21 years old. He wrote the letter.
Better: Jerry, a 21-year-old college student, wrote the letter.

- Sentence checklist:

All your sentences are complete sentences.

All sentence fragments have been eliminated.

No run-on sentences are used.

Short sentences with related ideas have been combined into longer sentences where appropriate.

PRACTICAL APPLICATIONS

1. During a community event or fair that has a police vehicle on display, ask the officer to demonstrate the departmental CAD system. Based on your readings, does it work as you thought it would?

2. If you were put in charge of automating a police department's records, what would be your recommendations? Draft a memorandum to the chief explaining how this automation should occur.

3. How many students in your class use computers to assist them in homework? Of that number, how many understand the operations of computers (including the following concepts)?

DOS
Windows
Programming a computer

4. In each of the rows below, circle the correctly spelled word:

stomoch	stomuch	stomach	stumoth
stencilled	stenciled	stencelied	stenceled
zeaulous	zeaulus	zealous	zealus
youthfull	youthful	youngful	youngfull
writen	writin	written	writtene
vegilance	vegilence	vigelance	vigilance
valueable	valeuable	valuable	vauleable
vitmin	vitamin	vitanim	vitamim
violator	violater	violeter	violatter
viwid	vivid	viwed	vived

5. Rewrite the following sentences as needed:

a. Jerry a ten year veteran was given the lifesaving reward then he retired.

_____

b. After shooting on the street all the witnesses was interviewed in the store.

_____

c. The officer entered the building and the officer searched every room.

_____

d. The victims car was black or red.

_____

e. The victim a prostitute was found in a ditch.

_____

6. Define and explain the following words or terms:

a. management information systems

_____

b. computer system

_____

c. NCIC

_____

d. NIBRS

_____

e. CAD

_____

WORDS TO KNOW

achievement	evidence
affirmative	genuine
altogether	judgment
analysis	liable
annual	maneuver
argument	noticeable
bicycle	oral
candidate	property
disabled	responsibility
disastrous	schedule

ENDNOTES

1. W. Lawrence Neurman and Bruce Wegand, *Criminal Justice Research Methods* (Needham Heights, MA: Allyn & Bacon, 2000) 462–463.

2. See Sheehan and Cordner, *Introduction to Police Administration,* 2d ed. (Ohio: Anderson, 1989), 417–419.

3. See G. Hobart Reiner, Thomas J. Sweeney, Ray V. Waymire, Fred A. Newton III, Richard G. Grassie, Susanne M. White, and William D. Wallaby, *Integrated Criminal Apprehension Program: Crime Analysis Operations Manual* (Washington, D.C.: GPO, Law Enforcement Assistance Administration, 1977), 1–9.

4. Michael D. Maltz, *Bridging Gaps in Police Crime Data* (Washington, D.C.; GPO, 1999).

5. Jan M. Chaiken, *Patrol Allocation Methology for Police Department* (Washington, D.C.: GPO, 1977).

6. For a set of standards dealing with intelligence files, see Standard 51.1.2, *Standards for Law Enforcement Agencies,* 2nd ed. (Fairfax, Va.: Commission on Accreditation for Law Enforcement Agencies, Inc., 1987), 51-1.

7. See Daniel L. Arkenau, "Records Management in the 1990s," *FBI Law Enforcement Bulletin* (June 1990): 16, for a discussion of optical disk image systems in the Cincinnati, Ohio, Police Department.

8. See Richard Rubin, "Computer Trends in Law Enforcement," *The Police Chief* (Apr. 1991): 20. This entire issue of *The Police Chief* provides an excellent source of information regarding computers and law enforcement.

9. K.W. Colton, M.L. Brandeau, and J.M. Tien, *A National Assessment of Police Command, Control, and Communications Systems* (Washington D.C.: National Institute of Justice, 1983).

10. See, Robert E. Scheetz, "Calling All Cars . . .," *The Police Chief* (July 1989): 61, and "Instant Playback of 911," *Law and Order* (Feb. 1994): 31, for discussions of an enhanced 911 system.

11. For a discussion of how to implement this type of computer program, see Mark Clark, "A Low-Cost Approach to High Technology," *FBI Law Enforcement Bulletin* (Nov. 1990): 8.

12. Information in this section was taken from William S. Sessions, "Compiling Law Enforcement Statistics from the 1920s to the 21st Century," *The Police Chief* (Oct. 1989): 10.

13. See Don M. Johnson, "NCIC Training Hit or Miss," *FBI Law Enforcement Bulletin* (Jan. 1991): 1.

14. This section is adapted from William S. Sessions, "Criminal Justice Information Services," *FBI Law Enforcement Bulletin* (Feb. 1993): 1.

10

Basic Reports

LEARNING OBJECTIVES

After reading this chapter, you should understand the following concepts:
- The different types of reports and their purposes.
- The information that is required when filling out a report.
- Why reports need to be accurate, complete, and fair.

KEY TERMS

Administrative reports—May be subdivided into two areas: (1) those that provide information concerning the agency's mission of protecting the public, and (2) those that set forth internal rules for the operation of the agency. The former documents are usually in the form of reports to the top-level management, and the latter documents involve procedures, orders, memorandums, or manuals that set forth departmental policy.

Annual report—Presents information concerning the operation of the department for the preceding year.

Case or crime report—Provides a written record of crimes reported to the police, including the details of the crime and the police action.

Daily report—An up-to-date report of the major crimes reported in the last 24 hours.

Follow-up or supplemental report—Sets forth information concerning any subsequent investigation and the results of that investigation.

General orders (GOs)—Administrative records utilized to pass information to lower level personnel within the department, rather than to set forth operational instructions.

Memo (memorandum)—Utilized to pass instruction or information from one party in the department to another.

Monthly report—Allows administrators to determine trends in both departmental functions and criminal behavior.

Offense report—The original record detailing facts surrounding the commission of a crime.

Operational records—Records directly connected with the apprehension and conviction of persons who commit crimes.

Special orders (SOs)—Specific orders that are temporary in nature.

Standard operating procedures (SOPs)—Administrative directives that establish a uniform procedure for the operation of the department in a certain area or situation.

Temporary operating procedures (TOPs)—Short-term directives for the operation of the department.

As indicated in other chapters, administrators utilize law enforcement reports when making decisions regarding departmental policies and missions. Individual police reports form the basis for decisions by policy makers. At the other end of the spectrum is the use of reports by officers when testifying in court. This aspect of report writing is examined in detail in Chapter 12. However, while court testimony is critical in convicting the offender, it is only one aspect of report writing. Law enforcement reports are used by individual officers in a number of ways: they are the principal source of information in conducting investigations, they provide the basis for transferring cases from one officer to another without loss of valuable information, and they are an accurate reflection of the individual officer's training, skill, and capabilities.[1]

Reports are important at all levels in law enforcement. There are many different types of reports. Each has a designated purpose. These various reports mandate different responses and efforts by the police officer who is writing them.[2] In addition, each law enforcement agency has its own particular rules and regulations regarding the writing of reports. This profusion of different rules, jurisdictions, and reports makes it difficult to set forth requirements that apply to each and every department and report. However, certain basic principles do apply to all law enforcement reports. In police report writing, there are two important types of reports. The next section discusses these two classifications of police records.

Common Errors in Report Writing

Listed below are the most common errors in report writing. Note that most of them are the result of oversights caused by simple carelessness.

1. Failure to provide sources of information.
2. Failure to report significant details.
3. Failure to write neatly and clearly.
4. The use of poor English.
5. Failure to maintain objectivity.

TYPES OF REPORTS

There are as many methods of classifying police records as there are law enforcement agencies. This is because there is no one single rigid system of reports that will work for every police department. However, general guidelines exist that can assist a police supervisor who is assigned the responsibility of administrating or establishing a records division.

While all police records are aimed at accomplishing the department's mission of protecting the public and preserving the peace, some records fall into the realm of general support: those records that assist in the administration of the department. Other records are operational—that is, they are directly connected to the apprehension and conviction of persons who commit crimes. This is therefore a commonsense and logical separation to make when examining police records.

Initial Police Reports

Often law enforcement agencies will require the use of special forms for initial police reports. While the reports vary among agencies, there are common practices to note. Normally, when the police receive a call for assistance or discover a crime, they are aware of the general nature of the misconduct. Accordingly, depending on the nature of the incident or crime, one of the following standard forms is used in reporting the incident:

- Case report
- Traffic citation
- Animal control violation
- Stolen vehicle report
- Arrest report
- Juvenile arrest report
- Stolen bicycle report
- Hit-and-run report
- Vehicle accident report
- Minor property damage accident report
- Petition for emergency commitment

The *case report,* or *crime report,* is used to provide a written record of crimes reported to the police, including details of the crime and the police action. The case report is generally used unless one of the previously listed special reports can be used. In some cases, both a case report and a special report are required.

In completing the case report, the preliminary investigator must determine if an offense has actually been committed by determining and documenting the elements of a crime. Often, reference to particular criminal codes is used to accurately describe the offense committed.

Case reports are generally coded in a manner that will alert the supervisor who reviews the reports as to the seriousness of the case.

Since the investigator on the scene generally has no information regarding the background of the suspects, standard case reports have a section to be completed by the department's records section after a records check has been made.

Operational Reports

Operational reports are directly connected with the apprehension and conviction of persons who commit crimes. The term *conviction* is included since part of the criminal justice system involves the officer testifying in court before a judge or jury. In almost all instances, the officer will rely on the written report prepared at the time of the incident. The officer may not have had anything to do with the arrest of the defendant, but testimony concerning the scene of the crime as recorded in the officer's report may be an essential part of the prosecutor's case and a necessary ingredient in the conviction of the defendant.

There are two distinct types of operational reports: the offense report and the follow-up or supplemental report. The *offense report* is the original record detailing facts surrounding the commission of a crime. The *follow-up* or *supplemental report* sets forth information concerning any subsequent investigation and the results of that investigation.

The preceding section briefly introduced the two primary types of operational reports utilized by a majority of law enforcement agencies. In addition, there are specialized operational reports that do not fit within this classification but should be considered as follow-up or supplementary reports. These reports concern the recording of such criminal activities as narcotics, intelligence, and, in some instances, sex cases. For the most part, offense reports do not initiate the investigation in these cases. Many of these types of crimes are handled by trained specialists who are involved in the case from the beginning to the trial of the offender.

Most of this text focuses on the operational aspects of policing and report writing. However, the cop on the street is unable to operate absent a formalized organizational structure. This structure, the police department, utilizes administrative reports to function.

Administrative Reports

Administrative reports are just as important as operational reports. Without administrative reports the department would grind to a halt and no law enforcement activities could be carried out.

Administrative reports can be subdivided into two areas: those that provide information concerning the agency's mission of protecting the public and those that set forth internal rules for the operation of the agency. The former documents are usually reports to top-level management; the latter documents involve procedures, orders, memorandums, or manuals that set forth departmental policy.

Following is a brief examination of administrative reports that establish internal rules within a department:

Standard Operating Procedures (SOPs)   These administrative records are directives that establish a uniform procedure for the operation of the department in a certain area or situation. They are normally established for an indefinite period of time and may be revised or updated depending on changed circumstances. Some departments have no SOPs, while others may have 100 or more. For example, the Los Angeles Police Department has over 100 SOPs. Standard operating procedures concern such operational matters as use of force, when an officer is authorized to go to Code 3 response (lights and siren), and other similar issues.

Temporary Operating Procedures (TOPs) These administrative records set forth short-term directives for the operation of the department. They differ from SOPs in that they have a specific starting and ending date. TOPs might be used to instruct departmental personnel on how to respond to an unusual event, such as the visit of an international dignitary or the arrival in the department's jurisdiction of a large outlaw motorcycle club. Unlike SOPs, temporary operating procedures have a definite termination date.

General Orders (GOs) These administrative records are utilized to pass information to lower level personnel within the department, rather than to set forth operational instructions. Additionally, general orders have traditionally been utilized to define or redefine the duties and responsibilities of officers. For instance, a GO might be issued that revises existing departmental policy and requires patrol officers to conduct a limited amount of the initial investigation of a crime before the case is referred to detectives. The basic distinction between GOs and SOPs is that SOPs are concerned with specific operational situations; GOs may affect the operations of a department, but they do so in an indirect manner. General orders may be utilized to pass information regarding court legal rulings or information received from another agency which requires coordination between that entity and the police department. This information then causes the officers to react differently in the field.

Special Orders (SOs) These orders are specific and temporary in nature. SOs are similar to general orders in that they are used to pass information rather than to dictate direct operational policy. They might be used to inform all personnel of transfers, promotions, or upcoming promotion examination dates.

Memos (memorandums) Memos are utilized to pass instructions or information from one party in the department to another. They may be of limited duration and are routinely utilized as a method of ensuring that all personnel understand the item being discussed. They are more effective than oral communications, especially when there are multiple districts and overlapping shifts. If the memo becomes a procedure it should be reformatted into a SOP or GO, depending on its content.

Duty Manual This administrative record is known by many names: procedures manual, department rules manual, operations manual, and so forth. This document has been defined as follows:

Duty manual: Describes procedures and defines the duties of officers assigned to specific posts or positions. . . . Duty manuals and changes in them should be made effective by general order; the changes should be incorporated into the first revision of the duty manual.[3]

All standard operating procedures and general orders should be included in the duty manual. In addition to containing a table of organization, duty manuals normally contain a job description for each departmental position. This establishes the duties and responsibilities of all members of the department. For example, the duty manual lists the responsibilities of a lieutenant assigned to patrol. The manual also lists the responsibilities of a lieutenant assigned to narcotics. As one can well imagine, the duties of these two lieutenants are substantially different.

The other form of administrative report provides information to high-level management regarding the operation of the department. The following three reports fall within this classification: (1) daily reports, (2) monthly reports, and (3) annual reports.

Daily Report This administrative record is utilized to present an up-to-date report of the major crimes reported in the last 24 hours. This report usually includes statistics showing the number of major crimes committed during the month to date, the number of major crimes committed during the year to date, and the number of major crimes committed in the last year up to the date of the report.

Daily reports also include information regarding the number of arrests for the same time periods. This report is an extremely effective tool for informing the chief of police and the department's upper management of the extent of criminal activity within their jurisdictions. The daily report serves as the basis for compiling the monthly and annual reports.

Monthly Report This report is a key management tool. While the daily report serves to keep the police administrator informed of the extent of criminal activity, the monthly report allows administrators to determine trends in both departmental functions and criminal behavior. For example, the monthly report may indicate a sudden rise in burglaries. This could alert the department to the need to adjust patrol boundaries within a district or might cause the burglary division to start inquiries on the street as to whether a new gang is operating in the area. The information contained in the monthly report forms the basis for the annual report.

Annual Report This report presents information concerning the operation of the department for the preceding year. It is considered an indispensable management tool in the profession.[4]

The preceding section described various types of police records which are found in most law enforcement agencies. The following sections examine the types of information that may be contained in these reports.

REQUIRED INFORMATION

As indicated previously, different reports are utilized for different purposes. However, all initial reports should contain certain building blocks of information. This information forms the basis for any arrest, follow-up investigation, and presentation of the case to the district attorney. This information can be classified under six separate headings: (1) *who,* (2) *what,* (3) *when,* (4) *where,* (5) *how,* and (6) *why.*

Who

Who is much broader than *who committed the crime.* This is an all-inclusive category that requires special attention by the responding officer. The question *who* is not answered by simply listing the name of the person suspected of committing the crime.

Who requires the officer to identify certain persons involved in the offense. *Who is the victim?* Many times, officers respond to a call and talk to a witness to a potential crime, but discover that finding the victim may be time consuming and, in some situations, futile.

Who is the offender? Is the person known to the victim, witness, or other persons? Can the officer obtain a name, description, or other information that may identify the offender?

Who are potential witnesses? Will they volunteer information, or are they afraid of retaliation by the offender? They should be identified by name, address, employment, and other information that will assist other officers if a follow-up or a second interview of the witnesses is required.

The officer must also ensure that law enforcement personnel who responded to the scene of the crime are identified. *Who was the first officer on the scene? Who conducted the investigation? Was any evidence collected and who was it turned over to?* All officers involved in the investigation must be identified and their roles explained.

Answering the question of *who* involves identifying the complaining party, victim, suspect, witnesses, and any involved law enforcement personnel. This identification should include residence and home addresses, telephone numbers, physical descriptions, and occupations where appropriate.

What

What is a broad question that covers a number of areas. The officer must ensure that all of these aspects are answered in any report. Many times citizens will call and report what they believe to be a certain type of crime. For example, a citizen may call and report being robbed. The officer who responds and interviews the victim may discover that the citizen has been the victim of a burglary instead of a robbery. Therefore, the type of offense reported and the offense actually committed may be different. Injuries, damage, or other physical aspects of the crime or the crime scene observed by the officer must be included in any report.

The officer must determine what evidence is available and what evidence was not obtained. The evidence may be oral, visual, or physical in nature. *What was done with any evidence?* Is there a chain of custody? Has it been properly marked, tagged, stored, and disposed of according to departmental policy and regulations?

The officer must also review what, if any, further police actions are required. *What agencies responded to the call? What agency assumed jurisdiction for the crime? What section or officers will conduct any necessary follow-up investigation?*

What type of offense was committed? Was it a crime against a person or property? An accident, natural disaster, or intentional act?

When

The question of *when* is more than the date, day, and time of the offense. The officer must examine this question from the perspectives of the offense, the citizens involved in the offense, and the law enforcement agency responding to the call for assistance. Each of these areas should be reviewed and basic information documented regarding when they became involved.

When was the offense committed or discovered? When was it reported? Was there a significant delay between discovery and reporting? If so, the officer needs to inquire into the reasons for this delay.

What persons were observed at the scene of the crime is a critical piece of information. What time did they arrive, how long did they stay, and when did they leave are questions and answers that should be sought by the officer. Was the victim at the scene or did he arrive at that location at a certain time? Did any witnesses have an opportunity to view the scene of the crime before the officers arrived? If so, what was the time and how long did they view the scene? Did they observe the incident? If so, for how long and from what location?

When did law enforcement officers arrive at the scene of the crime? How much time had passed since the commission of the crime, the report of the crime, and the arrival of the police? *When did the officer contact the victim, witnesses, or other parties and take their statements?* Recording this information may be critical if the victim or witness later changes the story. The fact that the officer obtained a statement within minutes, hours, or days immediately after the incident when the crime was fresh in their minds may become important in court if the witness or victim testifies differently during trial.

Where

This area of inquiry must cover the offense, persons involved in the incident, and police agencies. The officer must answer questions regarding the location of all these variables in the police report.

The most obvious question to be asked is *where was the offense committed?* The officer should not automatically assume that the location of the property or body is where the offense occurred. Where the offense was discovered may be different from where it took place. Where any crime occurred, was discovered, and where it was reported may be three distinct locations. The officer should ensure that any report clearly indicates the location and type of activity involved: *where the crime occurred, where it was discovered,* and *where it was reported.*

The location should be described by street address, intersection, or exact location in any building. What is the difference between a living room and a family room? The officer should ensure that the location is clear and understandable by any person who reads the report.

The officer should ensure that all available information is obtained regarding persons involved in the incident. The locations of the victim, witnesses, and suspect are critical to any investigation. Where they reside, their work addresses, all phone numbers, and other information necessary to contact them should be gathered and recorded by the officer. In addition, the location of all the parties at the time of the crime is important. Exactly where they were located may have a significant impact on their testimony. For example, a witness who was located across the street may not have been able to observe the color of the suspect's eyes.

The locations and activities of the police should be carefully recorded. Where they interviewed victims, witnesses, and suspects is important. Where they arrested the suspect may become critical. If it was inside a residence, did they have a warrant? Where evidence was observed, marked, and stored is important to follow-up investigators. Simply listing where the crime occurred is only the beginning of answering this query.

How

How the offense was committed is important for modus operandi files. What tools were used and how they were used are often critical pieces of evidence that may tie the offense into other similar crimes. *How was the offense discovered? How was it reported?*

How various persons were involved in the crime is often overlooked by inexperienced officers. *How was the victim transported to the hospital? How did the suspect arrive and depart the scene of the crime? How did witnesses happen to be at the location of incident?*

How police agencies responded at the scene of the crime is also important. *How did the officer identify the victim, suspect, and witnesses? How did they locate these individuals?*

Why

Motive, or *why a person commits a crime,* is not traditionally one of the elements of any offense. However, prosecutors and jurors want to know why the crime was committed; therefore, officers should attempt to answer this question if possible. *Why was the offense reported?* Was it for insurance purposes, to seek revenge, or other reasons? *Why did the suspect commit the crime in that manner?* Was there an easier method to accomplish the crime, and why didn't the suspect use it? *Why did witnesses come forward?* Is there any bias, prejudice, or motive to their cooperation?

As the preceding discussion indicates, there are several different ways of asking the same question. If the officer approaches report writing in this method, it will ensure that there is no gap or missing piece of information in the report. Simply put, gathering information is only the first step in writing a complete report. Once the information is obtained, the officer must organize it. The organization and structure of police reports is the subject of the next section.

ORGANIZATION OF REPORTS

All departments or agencies have standard forms that assist the officer in organizing and writing reports. Many of these reports have boxes or spaces for specific information regarding the crime and further information gathered by the officer. This format is to ensure consistency and completeness in law enforcement reports. However, after the first page of these reports is filled in, the officer is expected to write a summary or detailed account of the crime. This requires that the answers gathered during the initial investigation be organized and set forth in a clear and readable fashion.

Drafting the Report

The officer must learn to quickly and accurately place the information obtained at the crime scene into a readable document. This report should flow logically and be a complete record of the officer's involvement. To accomplish this the officer should utilize four principles in drafting any report: (1) start at the beginning, (2) write in chronological order, (3) place details in supplemental reports, and (4) write in the past tense. By using these principles, the officer will avoid leaving out valuable information and ensure that any person reading the report will understand what occurred.

The officer should begin any summary or narrative with his or her initial involvement: "Responded to a call for assistance," and so forth. This sets the stage for the reader to follow the officer's actions from the beginning to the end of the report. It also establishes when the officer became involved in the incident.

The officer should then proceed to write the report in chronological order. Starting at the beginning, the officer can proceed to the present time or the end of the report. This principle gives an easy order to the material and also ensures that the officer does not forget some item of information that might be left out if the report jumped from the beginning to the end and back to the middle of the officer's involvement.

General Rules on Report Writing

1. Law enforcement reports are generally written about past events. Accordingly, under most circumstances they should be written in the past tense. Rather than write that the car is black, state that the car was black. (It may have been repainted since that time.)

2. Be specific in quantifying an individual's behavior in your reports. While the subject may be "aggressive" or "combative," those words have different meanings to different people. For example, reporting that the subject "took a boxer's stance, tightened his lips across his teeth, was breathing rapidly, and brought up clenched fists" is a better description of the subject's conduct than the comment that the subject was "combative."

3. The officer writing the report should write in the first person. Report writing should be similar to speaking. When speaking to a colleague, you would not say "this officer." The third-person "fly on the wall" report is more cumbersome to write and not as easy to grasp for officers being trained in how to write reports.

4. When you are writing reports that contain statements of others (witnesses, suspects, or other officers) use the third person to refer to the others. "Officer Smith stated that the weapon belonged to him."

5. Use complete sentences in your report. All sentences should have subjects and verbs and convey complete thoughts. Do not write in sentence fragments. Sentence fragments are groups of words that begin with capital letters and end with periods but are not complete sentences.

6. If the subject is singular, the verb in that sentence should also be singular. If the subject is plural, the verb must also be pural.

7. Collective nouns are always singular, therefore their verbs should also be singular.

8. Indefinite pronouns are always singular.

9. Use adjectives to alter, give additional meaning to, or modify nouns and pronouns. Use adverbs to alter, give additional meaning to, or modify verbs, adjectives, and other adverbs.

10. Most words ending in *-ly* are adverbs. *Not, never,* and *very* are adverbs.

11. When deciding whether to use an adjective or an adverb, find the word being modified. If the word is a noun or pronoun, use an adjective. If the word is an adjective or adverb, use an adverb.

12. Do not use run-on sentences. Run-on sentences are sentences that contain two or more sentences in one long sentence.

13. Eliminate comma splices. Comma splices occur when two complete sentences are joined with commas without connecting words such as *and* or *but.*

14. Use correct punctuation in your reports. Poorly punctuated reports can be confusing and misleading.

15. Use apostrophes to show possession. Possessive pronouns (e.g., *his, hers, ours, yours, theirs,* and *its*) do not need apostrophes.

16. Many people do not understand the rules for using brackets. Accordingly, as a general rule do not use them in law enforcement reports.

17. Use quotation marks in reports only to enclose exactly what a person said.

18. Do not use abbreviations in reports that can be confusing to people who are unfamiliar with the subject matter. When in doubt, spell it out.

19. Poor spelling creates doubt about the report. One method of eliminating misspelling is through your choice of words.

20. If any force is used, the report should contain all the specifics of how and why the officer used force.

21. If handcuffs are used, the officer should report that fact. For example, one career law enforcement officer recommends the use of language similar to the following:

> Mr. Jones submitted to my handcuffing him. He was handcuffed with his hands behind his back with his palms facing outward. I then checked the handcuffs to see that the handcuffs were on properly and double-locked the handcuffs and checked that they were double-locked. I asked Mr. Jones how the handcuffs felt and he did not reply to my question. I placed the tip of my right little finger between each of Mr. Jones's wrists and the handcuffs were on properly (Edward Nowicki, "Report Writing: Keep Excessive Force Litigation at Bay," *Police* (Nov., 1999): 48).

The officer should cover only the main points in the initial report. Other details should be placed in supplemental or follow-up reports. This allows the reader to gain a quick understanding of the incident without getting bogged down in details. In addition, the officer is able to concentrate on explaining exactly what happened without weaving numerous details into the report. Details are important and may be critical in solving the case or convicting the offender. However, they belong in supplemental reports rather than the initial crime report.

The officer should write the report in the past tense since it has already occurred. This also assists the officer in maintaining the chronological order of events.

Format

As indicated previously, most law enforcement agencies have standard forms that the officer will use in drafting reports. Filling in these forms is relatively simple. Unfortunately, there is not an accepted form for all reports in the United States. However, the different forms used by various agencies normally include the following sections.

Front Sheet This is a preprinted form with short empty spaces, boxes that are checked, and space for short names, addresses, and other information. This portion of the report is relatively easy to fill out, since it requires the officer to fill in the blanks and limits the choice to a few common selections.

The front sheet is used by the records section to maintain statistical information about the type and number of crimes within the jurisdiction. It also provides any reader with a quick summary of the parties, the nature of the crime, and other pertinent information.

Narrative Section This is a blank portion of the report that is used by the officer to flesh out the front sheet information. It provides a chronological history of the officer's involvement.

The officer should follow the principles set forth previously in drafting the report in this section. It must be clear, concise, and understandable. This section does not include every conceivable detail about the crime. Within the narrative section, the officer will refer to other portions of the report or separate supplemental reports for more detail or information.

Conclusions and Recommendations This is the section that allows the officer to express opinions and/or recommend a course of action. At this point the officer may state, "Recommend case be referred to the D.A. for filing of P.C. 459 [burglary]." This is the officer's opinion or conclusion that a crime has been committed and that further action is necessary.

In addition to the three basic portions of any police report, there are three other sections that many departments include in initial reports. These are separate sections that detail witnesses' statements, property involved, and evidence collected by the officer or other officers.

Witness Statements This section sets forth any witness statements. Whenever possible, the officer should use direct quotes and not substitute words for those of the witness. The officer must ensure that facts are separated from opinions in this section. The witness may state, "I heard two loud sounds." The officer should record that statement and not substitute "I heard two gunshots." If the witness states, "I heard two shots," the officer should follow up with questions as to why the witness knew or recognized the sounds as gunfire. This adds to the witness's creditability and saves everyone embarrassment later.

Property This supplement is used to describe any property that was stolen or damaged. The property should be listed separately and described in detail. For example, if the property stolen was a man's watch, *one man's watch* does not fully identify the property. A more complete description would be: *One man's yellow gold watch, Balwin, Model No. 334, Serial No. 55555.*

The nature and extent of any injury to the property should be explained in detail. If photographs were taken, refer to them and where they are located; for

INITIAL CRIME REPORT

HARRISBURG POLICE BUREAU

☐ CRIMES AGAINST PERSONS   ☐ CRIMES AGAINST PROPERTY

1. UCR NO.	2. SECTION NO.	3. NAME OF CRIME	4. DATE OF INCIDENT	5. TIME INCIDENT OCC.	6. INCIDENT NO.
			MO. DATE YEAR DAY		

7. REPORT GRID	8. WEATHER	9. STATUS	10. EXACT LOCATION	11. DATE OF REPORT	12. TIME OF REPORT	13. DA NO.
	☐ RAIN ☐ SNOW ☐ CLEAR ☐ CLOUDY ☐ OTHER TEMP_____	☐ EXCEPTIONAL CLEARANCE ☐ CLEARED ☐ OPEN UNFOUNDED	☐ INSIDE ☐ OUTSIDE MO. DATE YEAR		Badge No.

14. REPORTED BY

15. NAME	16. RESIDENCE ADDRESS	17. CITY	18. STATE
☐ MR. ☐ MRS. ☐ MISS.	19. TELEPHONE 20. R/S/A 21. DATE/TIME DISCOVERED 22. CODE		
23. BUSINESS ADDRESS	24. CITY 25. STATE 26. TELEPHONE 27. OCCUPATION		

28. COMPLAINANT

29. NAME	30. RESIDENCE ADDRESS	31. CITY	32. STATE
☐ MR. ☐ MRS. ☐ MISS.	33. TELEPHONE 34. R/S/A 35. CODE 35A. WORK HOURS		
36. BUSINESS ADDRESS	37. CITY 38. STATE 39. TELEPHONE 40. OCCUPATION		

41. C COMPLAINANT

42. NAME	43. RESIDENCE ADDRESS	44. CITY	45. STATE
☐ MR. ☐ MRS. ☐ MISS.	46. TELEPHONE 47. R/S/A 48. CODE 48A. WORK HOURS		
49. BUSINESS ADDRESS	50. CITY 51. STATE 52. TELEPHONE 53. OCCUPATION		

54. VICTIM NO. 1

55. NAME	56. RESIDENCE ADDRESS	57. CITY	58. STATE
☐ MR. ☐ MRS. ☐ MISS.	59. TELEPHONE 60. R/S/A 61. CODE 62. WORK HOURS		
63. BUSINESS ADDRESS	64. CITY 65. STATE 66. TELEPHONE 67. OCCUPATION		

68. NO. OF OFFENDERS COMPLETE SUSPECTS PORTION	69. HOW & WHERE ENTERED	70. HOW AND WHERE EXIT MADE	71. FORCE USED ☐ YES ☐ NO	72. TYPE OF WEAPON/FORCE	73. CRIME SCENE SEARCHED ☐ YES ☐ NO

74. PRINTS TAKEN ☐ YES ☐ NO BY:	75. PHOTOGRAPHS TAKEN ☐ YES ☐ NO BY:	76. TYPE OF PREMISES ☐ HOME ☐ OFFICE ☐ APT. ☐ OTHER	77. PREMISES PROTECTED BY ALARM ☐ YES ☐ NO

78. TYPE OF INJURY (DESCRIBE IN NARRATIVE)	79. CONDITION OF VICTIM ☐ GOOD ☐ FAIR ☐ POOR ☐ DECEASED	80. NEXT OF KIN NOTIFIED ☐ YES ☐ NO	81. CORONER NOTIFIED ☐ YES ☐ NO	82. DA. NOTIFIED ☐ YES ☐ NO	83. HOSPITAL AND/OR DOCTOR TAKEN TO

WAS THERE A WITNESS TO CRIME?

84. WITNESS

86. NAME	87. RESIDENCE ADDRESS	88. CITY	89. STATE
☐ MR. ☐ MRS. ☐ MISS.	90. TELEPHONE 91. R/S/A 92. CODE		
93. BUSINESS ADDRESS	94. CITY 95. STATE 96. TELEPHONE 97. OCCUPATION		

98. WITNESS

99. NAME	100. RESIDENCE ADDRESS	101. CITY	102. STATE
☐ MR. ☐ MRS. ☐ MISS.	103. TELEPHONE 104. R/S/A 105. CODE		
106. BUSINESS ADDRESS	107. CITY 108. STATE 109. TELEPHONE 110. OCCUPATION		

CODES:
1. ARRESTED
2. INCARCERATED
3. OUT ON BAIL
4. INTERVIEWED
5. NOT AVAILABLE FOR INTERVIEW

6. DOES NOT WISH TO BE INTERVIEWED OR INVOLVED
7. WILLING TO PROSECUTE
8. NOT WILLING TO PROSECUTE
9. RECOMMENDED TO BE SUPONEAD FOR COURT
10. SOBER (5)

11. HAD BEEN DRINKING (HBD)
12. INTOXICATED (I)
13. ON CONTROLLED SUBSTANCE (OCS)
14. ACCUSED BEING SOUGHT
15. CAN MAKE POSITIVE IDENTIFICATION OF ACCUSED OR SUSPECT
16. MENTALLY DISTURBED

POLICE 22/FORM1

INCIDENT NO.		EXISTENCE OF A SIGNIFICANT MO IDENTIFICATION OF SUSPECT		☐☐☐☐		☐☐☐☐	
☐ SUSPECT ☐ ACCUSED						☐	

110. NAME ☐ MR. ☐ MRS. ☐ MISS	111. ADDRESS	112. R/S/A	113. HT.	114. WT.	115. CODE
116. OTHER CHARACTERISTICS					

A. SUSPECT NAME OR GOOD DESCRIPTION   B. KNOWLEDGE OF SUSPECT LOCATION   A. ☐   B. ☐

☐ SUSPECT   ☐ ACCUSED

118. NAME ☐ ☐ ☐	119. ADDRESS	120. R/S/A	121. HT.	122. WT.	123. CODE
124. OTHER CHARACTERISTICS					

PRESENCE OF A DESCRIPTION WHICH IDENTIFIES THE VEHICLE USED BY THE SUSPECT   ☐

125. VEHICLE	126. NAME	127. TYPE	128. COLOR	129. YEAR OF VEHICLE	130. REGISTRATION NO. & STATE
	131. OTHER CHARACTERISTICS		132. OWNER		

133. OWNER ADDRESS	134. TOWED TO		
135. TOWED BY	136. VEHICLE INVENTORIED ☐ YES ☐ NO	136A PROPERTY RECORD SHEET COMPLETED ☐ YES ☐ NO	137. DATE

A LIMITED OPPORTUNITY TO COMMIT THE CRIME

A LIMITED NUMBER OF PERSONS AS POSSIBLE SUSPECTS

BELIEF THAT A CRIME CAN BE SOLVED WITH REASONABLE INVESTIGATIVE EFFORT

BELIEF THAT A CRIME CAN BE SOLVED WITH PUBLICITY

PRESENCE OF SIGNIFICANT PHYSICAL EVIDENCE

PROPERTY WITH IDENTIFIABLE CHARACTERISTICS, MARKS OR NUMBERS WHICH CAN BE TRACED

POSITIVE RESULTS FROM A CRIME SCENE EVIDENCE SEARCH

NARRATIVE: DESCRIBE IN FURTHER DETAIL ANY CONTENTS PLACED IN BLOCKS, SUCH AS WEAPONS USED, HOW THEY WERE USED, ETC. DESCRIBE MEANS OF ATTACK, DIRECTION IN WHICH SUSPECT(S) FLED, FURTHER TRADEMARKS OF OTHER DISTINGUISHING POINTS OF SUSPECT. GIVE STATEMENTS OF VICTIMS, WITNESSES, SUSPECTS, AND THEIR LOCATION AT THE TIME OF THE CRIME. EXPLAIN FACTS OF ARREST--SUMMARIZE CHRONOLOGICAL DETAILS OF OFFENSE, OBSERVATIONS MADE AT THE SCENE, ETC. GIVE ITEMS RECOVERED IN GENERAL TERMS AND PLACED ON PROPERTY RECORD. (USE ADDITIONAL SHEETS OF 8 1/2 X 11 PAPER IF NECESSARY).

138. CASE CLOSED ☐ YES ☐ NO	139. ARREST(S) MADE ☐ YES ☐ NO	139A. WITNESS SHEET ATTACHED ☐ YES ☐ NO	139B. PROBABLE CAUSE AFFIDAVIT ATTACHED ☐ YES ☐ NO	140. FURTHER ARREST(S) TO BE MADE ☐ YES ☐ NO	141. CONTINUATION REPORT ATTACHED ☐ YES ☐ NO	142. RECOMMEND DET ASSIGN ☐ YES ☐ NO
143. RECOMMEND YOUTH AID ASSIGN ☐ YES ☐ NO	144. RECOMMEND COM. RELA. ASSIGN ☐ YES ☐ NO	145. RECOMMEND SERVICES DIVISION ASIGN ☐ YES ☐ NO	146. RECOMMEND PAT ASSIGN ☐ YES ☐ NO	147. FOLLOW UP NECCESSARY ☐ YES ☐ NO	148. SERVICE BY SUMMONS REQUIRED ☐ YES ☐ NO	149. COMPLAINT (TYPING NEEDED) ☐ YES ☐ NO
150. TYPING BY: COMPLETED ☐ YES ☐ NO	151. STATEMENT, CONFESSION ATTACH ☐ YES ☐ NO	152. CRIME PREVENTION INFO REQUESTED ☐ YES ☐ NO	152A. VICTIMS/WITNESS HANDBOOK DISTRIBUTED ☐ YES ☐ NO	153. SECURITY SURVEY REQUESTED ☐ YES ☐ NO	OFFICER'S FULL NAME	BADGE NO.
SUPERVISOR'S FULL NAME			BADGE NO.	DATE		

☐ I FULLY AGREE WITH THE CONTENTS OF THIS REPORT

☐ I DO NOT AGREE WITH THE CONTENTS OF THIS REPORT   POLICE22/FORM | ENTERED BY |

example, *photographs attached* or *photographs taken and maintained by crime lab personnel, contact Technician Smith.*

Evidence This section refers to any evidence obtained during the investigation. It should be itemized, identified, and its locations listed. If possible, photographs or photocopies of any physical evidence should be attached to the report.

All of this information is critical, to allow other officers to continue any follow-up investigation. It provides a standard format and flow of information that is easy to understand and ensures that vital information is not omitted. The next section examines the content of any law enforcement report.

CONTENT

This section does not discuss how to write the numerous reports required of law enforcement officers; rather, it explains how that information should be set forth. As indicated in previous chapters, police reports serve a variety of purposes. To meet these various objectives, they are read, reviewed, and acted on by different individuals and agencies. It is therefore necessary that any police report contain all the necessary information. Police reports must be *accurate, complete,* and *fair.*[5] The following sections will discuss each of these concepts.

Accuracy

Accuracy in a police report requires that it be written in an objective manner. The officer must verify information contained in the report. An item as simple as the date versus the day can be critical in a police report.

Accurate reports must be clear and understandable. Spelling, grammar, and sentence structure add to the accuracy of any report. Use of correct grammar ensures that the reader understands what the officer is attempting to communicate. The difference between *there* and *their* may not seem like a major mistake to a civilian, but it can make a difference in a police report.

Accuracy also implies that the report is turned in to the department in a timely manner. Adding information to the initial report after it has been filed is unacceptable. If additional information is discovered after the initial report has been completed, the officer should submit a supplemental report and explain why the information was not included in the initial report.

Completeness

All police reports should be complete. The reader should be able to pick up any initial report and answer all the questions listed previously. While the report must be complete, the officer must not be so detail oriented as to confuse the reader. Therefore, completeness includes the principle of *conciseness.*

The officer must learn when to leave information in the main body of the report and when to place it in a supplemental report. The report cannot be so brief and full of references that the reader must constantly flip back and forth between different attachments. Additionally, the report should not be so lengthy and full of details that the reader must wade through the unimportant to find the useful information.

Fairness

It is difficult, but the officer must constantly keep in mind the obligations to be fair to everyone involved in the criminal justice system. This includes the suspect. The officer is not an advocate for one side or another. As Joe Friday of *Dragnet* fame used to say, "Just the facts" really applies to report writing.

Fairness in a police report requires combining accuracy and completeness to ensure that all relevant information is reported. The officer's credibility and reputation will outlive any single report; therefore, their integrity should never be compromised on any case.

The report should clearly distinguish between facts, inferences, opinions, and judgments. *Facts* are those items that can be independently verified. Facts are information the officer has obtained or observed. *Inferences* are suppositions of what "probably" occurred. These are statements the officer makes which are drawn from facts. Personal *opinions* of the officer are personal beliefs and should never be placed in a report. However, the officer may place the personal opinions of witnesses or victims in the report so long as they are clearly indicated to be opinions and not facts. The officer's personal approval or disapproval of certain acts are considered *judgments* and do not belong in police reports.

SUMMARY

Every agency has its own special rules for writing reports. However, many agencies incorporate certain basic principles or require the same or similar information in their reports. Every law enforcement officer must understand how to approach the report-writing task. Like many other personal skills, effective report writing is achieved only with practice and a conscious effort to improve.

All reports should contain the basic information necessary for supervisors to make informed decisions. This information includes *who, what, when, where, how,* and *why*. This information is necessary for a variety of reasons, including modus operandi, follow-up investigation, and departmental use.

Officers must ensure that all reports are *accurate, complete,* and *fair.* As will be discussed in other chapters, the credibility of the officer may depend on his or her ability to write an intelligent report. Report writing is probably one of the least favorite and most avoided activities in a police agency. However, the benefit of a well-written police report may be the conviction of a violent criminal.

REVIEW QUESTIONS

1. What is the most important fact in any report—*who, what, when, where, how,* or *why?* Justify your answer.

2. If why a person commits a crime is not part of the elements of the crime, why should police officers be required to spend their time attempting to answer this question?

3. Which of the four principles of drafting is the most important? Why? If you had to eliminate one of these principles, which one would you choose? Why?

4. Explain why departments have separate reports for different aspects of a crime, such as a separate sheet for witness statements.

5. The section dealing with content lists three basic areas that all police report writers should ensure are present—*accuracy, completeness,* and *fairness.* Which is the most important and why?

BETTER WRITING DRILLS

Becoming a Speedy Writer

The purpose of this section is to help you develop a comfortable style of writing and help make you a speedy and correct writer. Too often we waste time by reacting to each situation as if it were new. If you develop certain habits in your writing style, you will gain in both speed and accuracy. Checklists become automatic, and you are less likely to leave essential items out of your report. A clear-cut plan for conducting and writing an investigative report will make your report easier to write, faster to read, and less likely to contain errors or omissions. The habits that you develop should normally include the following:

1. Always use checklists. For example, develop checklists on specific crimes.

2. Form habits regarding your method of referring to yourself, how you refer to others, and your method of describing others.

3. Form habits regarding your system for listing and describing evidence and other items.

4. Form habits for your methods of checking and describing places, locations, trademarks, and MOs.

5. Be objective. Descriptions should be of observations rather than interpretations. For example, if a person is limping, indicate that the person was limping. Do not describe the individual as having a broken foot or a sprained ankle.

6. Get into the habit of placing in quotes all word-for-word statements made by individuals. Make sure that the report clearly identifies the individuals making the statements.

7. Always list your sources of information in your report. For example, . . . *according to witness Black, "Jones threw the first punch."*

8. Do not use long, complicated sentences. Reports are written to provide information, not to entertain the reader.

People How should you refer to yourself? How should you refer to others? Unless your agency dictates to you regarding these questions, make your choice and stick to it. The present trend is to always refer to yourself in the first person. Always describe others in the same way, in a preset order, and use a checklist. For example, always describe a person from head to foot. Use a checklist that includes name, sex, age, height, weight, build, address, phone, occupation, business address, home address, clothing, and so forth.

Property Use checklists to describe the various types of property. For example, in describing an automobile start with license, make, model or type, year, color, and peculiarities.

Places Often, people are not specific enough when describing places. Do not assume that a street address is sufficient. If possible, include room numbers, apartment numbers, and so forth. Make it a habit to be precise in describing locations of incidents. Get into the habit of describing a location in a standard, sequential method. For example, if you always survey a room from left to right, always describe it in the same way.

PRACTICAL APPLICATIONS

1. Select a class that you are attending. On a specific date, record your activities and observations from the time you enter the class until you leave it. Describe what occurred and, using the principles set forth in this chapter, draft a complete initial crime report.

2. Pick two other students in your class and describe any jewelry they are wearing. After you have written the description, ask them to comment on its accuracy. If you were given this description, could you locate that property?

3. Change each of the following statements from an interpretation to an observable fact:

   Jerry Jones was angry.

   Harry Smith was ill.

   Jerry wanted to leave.

   Sue Walton had a broken leg.

4. Each of the following sentences was taken from a police report. Write a question that arises in your mind when you read each sentence.

   The middle suspect was caught by automobile.

   The accused was uncooperative and angry.

The suspect indicated that he wished to leave.

The subject engaged in a verbal dispute with the other subject.

5. In each of the rows below, circle the correctly spelled word:

questionaire	questioneaire	questionnere	questionnaire
quantity	quantety	quantitiy	quanitity
stanard	standerd	standard	stendard
punisheble	pusnishable	punishble	punishable
singuler	singeler	singular	singlar
separete	saparate	separete	separate
suffocation	suffacation	sufocation	suffocatione
sucessful	succesfull	successful	successfull
strungulation	strunglation	stranglation	strangulation
stifening	stifenent	stiffening	stifen

6. Rewrite the following sentences as needed:

a. Because it was written without any support it is an opinion and should not be used in the report, next try to include the key facts.

_____

b. In view of the fact that he was only five years out of school I did not believe him.

_____

c. The two suspects got into a physical altercation and then into a fight.

_____

d. This officer responded to the accident scene quick.

_____

e. I advised the suspect who spoke only Spanish of his rights in English.

_____

7. Define and explain the following words or terms:

a. daily report

_____

b. special orders

_____

c. TOPs

_____

d. SOPs

_____

e. initial police report

_____

WORDS TO KNOW

automatic	perform
awkward	personnel
conspicuous	statistics
courteous	supersede
disappear	theft
disturbance	together
humane	toxicology
legible	traverse
nevertheless	vehicle
opportunity	weird

ENDNOTES

1. Michael T. D'Aulizio, "Instituting Quality Control Measures for Police Reports," *The Police Chief* (Oct. 1992): 129–132.

2. Myron Miller and Paula Pomerenke, "Police Reports Must Be Reader Based," *Law and Order* (Sept. 1989): 66–69.

3. O. W. Wilson, *Police Administration* (New York: McGraw-Hill, 1963), 33.

4. Jerome R. Wolff, "The Police Department Annual Report," *The Police Chief* (Apr. 1980): 22.

5. For an excellent discussion of the purposes of basic police reports, see "Records—Part III," *International Association of Chiefs of Police Training Key Series No. 198* (Alexandria, Va., 1973).

11

Interviews and Interrogations

LEARNING OBJECTIVES

After reading this chapter, you should understand the following concepts:
- The difference between an interview and an interrogation.
- The rationale for requiring *Miranda* warnings to be given to suspects of crimes.
- The different techniques used by police when questioning a witness to a crime.
- How to interview a crime victim.
- The various techniques police use when questioning a suspect.

KEY TERMS

Interrogation—Systematic questioning of an individual *who is in custody or is deprived of freedom in any significant way* for the purpose of gathering information regarding an actual or suspected crime.

Interview—Systematic questioning of an individual to gather information regarding an actual or suspected crime.

Post-traumatic stress disorder—The development of characteristic symptoms following a psychologically distressing event that is outside the range of usual human experience.

INTRODUCTION

Interviews and *interrogations* are unique forms of communication that usually occur only in a law enforcement agency. These information-gathering techniques are critical in apprehending and obtaining criminal convictions. They are distinguished from each other by purpose and the circumstances surrounding the collection of the desired information.

An *interview* is a systematic questioning of an individual to gather information regarding an actual or suspected crime. An *interrogation* is a systematic questioning of an individual *who is in custody or is deprived of freedom in any significant way* for the purpose of gathering information regarding an actual or suspected crime. As the preceding definitions indicate, the difference between the two types of inquiry centers on the fact that during an interrogation the person is not free to leave. The following sections examine, compare, and contrast the interview and the interrogation and analyze special issues that arise concerning a law enforcement officer's communication skills.

MIRANDA AND ITS EFFECT

Before the U.S. Supreme Court decided *Miranda v. Arizona,* confessions and the accompanying interrogations were decided on a case-by-case basis. This approach reviewed the circumstances surrounding the interrogation to determine if the suspect's will was broken by the police. The interrogation was considered improper if it violated the suspect's due process rights.

Pre-*Miranda* Techniques

In *Brown v. Mississippi,* the defendant was taken to the crime scene, where he was questioned regarding his involvement in a murder.[1] After denying guilt, he was hung by a rope from a tree. He continued to claim innocence and was tied to the tree and whipped. He was released, but was subsequently again seized and whipped until he finally confessed. The court held that the interrogation and confession were products of *coercion* and brutality and violated the defendant's Fourteenth Amendment due process rights.

In *Ashcraft v. Tennessee,* the defendant was taken to the police station and questioned continuously for two days regarding the murder of his wife.[2] The officers questioned Ashcraft in relays because they became exhausted during the interrogation; however, the defendant was denied rest and sleep during the entire time. The court held that the prolonged interrogation of Ashcraft was coercive and, therefore, the confession was *involuntary* and inadmissible.

In *Spano v. New York,* the defendant was suspected of a murder.[3] Spano informed a friend, who was a rookie police officer, that he had in fact killed the victim. Spano was arrested, and the rookie officer was instructed to tell Spano that he was in trouble and might lose his job unless Spano confessed. Spano finally confessed to the killing. The Supreme Court held that the use of deception as a means of psychological pressure to obtain a confession was a violation of the defendant's constitutional rights; therefore, the confession was ruled *involuntary* and was suppressed.

In *Escobedo v. Illinois,* the defendant was arrested for murder and interrogated for several hours at the police station.[4] During the interrogation, Escobedo repeatedly requested to see his attorney—who was also at the police station, demanding to see his client. The police refused both requests and finally obtained the confession. The court held that Escobedo was denied his right to counsel and, therefore, no statement obtained from him could be used at a criminal trial.

Escobedo was confusing because it was unclear when this right to counsel attached during the interrogation. Trial courts began interpreting the meaning of *Escobedo* differently. Thus, the stage was set for the U.S. Supreme Court to clear up the confusion that resulted from its previous rulings.

Miranda

In *Miranda v. Arizona,* the U.S. Supreme Court established certain safeguards for individuals who are being interrogated by police.[5] Most people know that the *Miranda* decision requires police officers to advise defendants of their constitutional rights. In reality, *Miranda* established a four-prong test that must be satisfied before a suspect's statements can be admitted into evidence. The test requires affirmative answers to all four of the following questions:

1. Was the statement voluntary?
2. Was the *Miranda* warning given?
3. Was there a waiver by the suspect?
4. Was the waiver intelligent and voluntary?

Unless all these questions are answered in the affirmative, none of the suspect's statements can be admitted into evidence. In *Miranda,* the defendant was arrested at home in Phoenix, Arizona, in connection with the rape and kidnapping of a female and was taken to a police station for questioning. At the time, he was 23, poor, and basically illiterate. After being questioned for two hours, he confessed to the crime. The Supreme Court issued its now-famous *Miranda* warning requirement, stating:

> We hold that when an individual is taken into custody or otherwise deprived of his freedom . . . , the privilege against self-incrimination is jeopardized. . . . He must be warned prior to any questioning that he has a right to remain silent, that anything he says can be used against him in a court of law, that he has a right to an attorney, and that if he cannot afford an attorney one will be appointed for him prior to any questioning if he so desires.

The *Miranda* decision drew a bright line for admissibility of confessions and admissions obtained during investigations. It changed the way police interrogate suspects. While the decision was sweeping in its scope, it still left questions unanswered.

In *Berkemer v. McCarty,* the Supreme Court held that the *Miranda* warning must be given during any custodial interrogation.[6] The court held that a person subjected to a custodial interrogation must be given the warning regardless of the severity of the offense, but questioning a motorist at a routine traffic stop does not constitute custodial interrogation.

The *Miranda* decision has generated both support and criticism since its inception. Supporters argue that it protects the rights of those accused of crimes, while detractors claim that it allows the guilty to go free because an officer may not have followed all the rules. In recent years, the courts have begun to allow statements to be admitted into evidence despite the absence of the *Miranda* warning.

The Eroding of *Miranda*

Miranda did not prevent statements obtained in violation of its rules from being used to impeach the credibility of a defendant who takes the witness stand. In *Harris v. New York,* the court held that it was proper to use such statements so long as the jury was instructed that the confession was not to be considered as evidence of guilt, but only to determine if the defendant was telling the truth.[7]

Voluntary statements made by the defendant without having received the *Miranda* warning are admissible, even though the defendant is later advised of his rights and waives those rights. In *Oregon v. Elstad,* the defendant was picked up at his home as a suspect in a burglary and made incriminating statements without receiving his *Miranda* warning.[8] After being advised of his rights, he waived them and signed a confession. The Supreme Court held that the self-incrimination clause of the Fifth Amendment did not require suppression of the written confession because of the earlier unwarned admission.

In *Illinois v. Perkins,* the Supreme Court held that an undercover officer posing as an inmate need not give a jailed defendant the *Miranda* warning before asking questions that produce incriminating statements.[9] The court held that there is no coercive atmosphere present when an incarcerated person speaks freely to someone whom he believes is a fellow inmate. The court added that the *Miranda* warning does not forbid strategic deception by taking advantage of a suspect's misplaced trust.

In *Arizona v. Fulminante,* the U.S. Supreme Court held that the harmless error rule is applicable to cases involving involuntary confessions.[10] The *harmless error rule* holds that an error made by the trial court in admitting illegally obtained evidence does not require a reversal of the conviction if the error was determined to be harmless. The burden of proving harmless error rests with the prosecution and must be proved beyond a reasonable doubt.

In *Davis v. United States,* the U.S. Supreme Court considered the degree of clarity that is necessary for a suspect to invoke his *Miranda* rights.[11] Agents of Naval Investigative Service were questioning the defendant in connection with the death of a sailor. He initially waived his rights, but approximately 90 minutes later stated, "Maybe I should talk to a lawyer." The agents asked clarifying questions; when the defendant stated that he did not want an attorney, the interrogation resumed, eliciting incriminating statements. The court held that an equivocal request for a lawyer is insufficient to invoke the right to counsel and that there is no need for clarifying questions before proceeding with the interrogation.

After years of allowing suspects to avoid police interrogation by invoking their *Miranda* rights, the Supreme Court is beginning to take a more reasonable and practical approach to this controversial issue.[12] Police officers must carefully tailor their interrogations so that they obtain information while at the same time protecting the suspect's constitutional rights.

INTERVIEWS

Interviews are a key part of any investigation. Various techniques are used during interviews to elicit information from the different types of witnesses. No single method will work for all officers or be effective on all witnesses. While the general rules regarding interviews also apply to crime victims, special consideration must be given to their needs and feelings. A successful interview is composed of tact, sensitivity, and determination.[13]

Interviewing Witnesses

A witness interview does not occur without preparation and hard work on the part of an officer. However, before a witness can be interviewed one must be found.

Identification of Witnesses One of the cardinal rules in law enforcement interviewing is to locate witnesses to a crime as soon as possible. There are several reasons for this principle. First, locating and interviewing witnesses immediately after the commission of the crime allows officers to broadcast the suspect's description to other officers. The greater the lapse of time from the incident to the witness interview, the greater the chance that the witness will not recall all that was observed. Another reason for interviewing witnesses as soon as possible after the crime is to prevent them from comparing stories with other witnesses and changing their accounts of what they saw.

Witnesses may be located in a number of different places; however, the crime scene is the most obvious place to begin. Normally, people who remain at crime scenes are willing to provide information to the police. The officer should approach the most obvious witness first; this will normally be someone who is excited or talkative. Avoid asking, "Did you see what happened?" A more open-ended question will elicit a wider response. A question such as "What happened here?" may lead to other witnesses. The first question may be answered by a simple "No," while the second question may provide other information: "I didn't see who fired the shot, but the janitor saw everything." Thus, the technique of how the initial question is posed may determine the citizen's answer or level of cooperation.

Officers should consider revisiting the crime scene on a daily basis for a week after the crime was committed. If at all possible, this visit should occur at the same time that the crime originally occurred. Pedestrians, schoolchildren, and other people who may have been in the area at the time of the crime should be questioned. The officer should approach these citizens with an understanding attitude and stress the need to cooperate with the police during this period of time.

A third technique in locating witnesses is canvassing the neighborhood. This normally occurs only after a serious crime, such as homicide, has been committed. Since this is a staff-draining exercise, the police administrator will be called on to justify this use of officers. When contacting neighbors, the officer should present identification, explain the reason for the visit, relate the time of the crime, and ask if the witness saw or heard anything unusual. If the answer is in the affirmative, the officer can then proceed to more specific questions regarding the crime.

Finally, the victim or suspect's friends or relatives should be interviewed in an attempt to locate witnesses. The officer should approach these citizens in a professional manner and begin the interview with open-ended, nonspecific questions. If one of these persons has any knowledge about either the victim or the suspect, the officer should then proceed to specific areas of inquiry. This allows the officer to develop a well-rounded picture of either the victim or the suspect. Identifying potential witnesses is the first step in the process of interviewing witnesses.

Interview Preparation The officer cannot always select the interview location. Therefore, the officer must rely on communication skills and control the communication process in order to elicit the needed information. The officer must have as much information as possible prior to conducting any interview. Depending on the situation, the officer may conduct the interview at the scene of the crime, at a witness's home, or at the police department. The officer should control the interview and ensure that critical items of information are obtained. At the same time, the officer must not be so rigid in questioning as to miss a witness's offhanded remark that might lead to information that will assist in the arrest of the suspect.

In situations where there are numerous distractions, the officer should attempt to obtain only the basic facts and should schedule a follow-up interview to gather other information. A basic description of the suspect, what the witness observed, and the witness's name, address, and both work and residence telephone numbers may be all the information the officer is able to obtain in these situations.

The follow-up interview is a vital phase of the interviewing process. The officer should review all available information prior to conducting this interview. The normal procedure for such an interview is to follow a structured or logical sequence of questioning. Random questioning is rarely used because it lacks direction and fails to obtain all pertinent information. Witnesses should be allowed to relay all the information in their possession before the officer begins to ask questions. When interrupted during a statement, a witness may forget a fact or pick up the narrative at a different point.

Preparation is critical to the efficient, productive interview of witnesses. The officer must be prepared for the interview by knowing the facts surrounding the incident. The officer must also know when and where a brief interview is appropriate and when a more thorough interview is necessary.

Conducting the Interview The actual interview should flow very smoothly if the officer has prepared properly. The officer must remember to remain courteous, attentive, and professional. If the witness is uncomfortable relating the facts of the incident, the officer should offer supportive comments. If the witness seems reluctant to talk, the officer can remind the witness of a citizen's obligations. An officer may use many techniques during the interview process but the primary duty is to make sure the lines of communication with the witness remain open.

Evaluating Witnesses One of the tasks of the interviewing officer is to evaluate the credibility of the witness. Credibility can be defined as the believability of the witness. In other words, what are the personal characteristics that render this witness's testimony worthy of belief by an impartial party? These characteristics include truthfulness, opportunity to observe, accuracy in reporting what was observed, and motive for testifying.

Four factors may determine credibility: (1) opportunity, (2) attention, (3) personal knowledge, and (4) physical characteristics. The officer should evaluate each of these factors when judging a witness's credibility.

> *Opportunity* refers to the witness's awareness of his surroundings. Was he in a location that allowed for an unobstructed view of the crime? Did he see only part of the act? Can he contribute facts that, although not specific to the crime, assist the investigators in putting together a complete picture of the incident?

> *Attention* requires that the witness be aware of the incident. What brought the event to the witness's attention? The witness may have paid attention to only part of the incident, and the officer must resist the temptation to put words in the witness's mouth regarding something that the witness did not observe. For example, if a witness states, "The first time I saw him was when he shoved the shotgun in the teller's face," the officer should not attempt to have the witness testify regarding when the suspect entered the bank.

> *Personal knowledge* relates to those facts that the witness observed or experienced. The officer should ensure that the witness actually observed what she states she saw, heard, or felt. To do this, the officer may want to determine where the witness was located in relation to the incident, the location of other persons, and any other facts which may show that the witness was where she states she was and that she had an unobstructed view of the scene of the crime.

> *Physical characteristics* concern the witness's ability to observe and relate what he saw. Does the witness wear glasses, contact lenses, a hearing aid? Is the witness color-blind? If so, is it critical to his testimony?

Once the interviewing is completed, the officer should compare the witnesses' statements against each other to assist in evaluating their credibility.

Successfully interviewing witnesses is more an art form than a science. However, general principles regarding the interview process will assist the officer in communicating with witnesses. Locating witnesses, preparing for the interview, conducting the interview, and evaluating the credibility of witnesses are necessary steps in this process.

Interviewing Victims

Many of the same techniques discussed in the preceding apply when interviewing victims of crimes. Victims are also witnesses to the crime in many situations. However, victims must be treated differently than witnesses for a variety of reasons.

Some victims will experience emotional or mental problems as a result of the crime. Many crime victimization studies have examined the effects of sexual assault on victims, but consensus is being developed among experts that victims of serious nonsexual crimes may also experience demonstrated psychological effects as a result of the offense.

Post-traumatic stress syndrome came into our consciousness as a result of the Vietnam War. Returning veterans reported flashbacks, severe depression, and other symptoms. Post-traumatic stress syndrome is now recognized as a mental disorder. There might be some confusion between the words *syndrome* and *disorder*. *Syndrome* connotes a collection of symptoms, while *disorder* is the clinical diagnostic term. The *Diagnostic Statistical Manual of Mental Disorders–IV* states that the essential feature of post-traumatic stress disorder (PTSD) is the development of characteristic symptoms following a psychologically distressing event that is outside the range of usual human experience. The victim usually experiences intense fear, terror, and helplessness. The characteristic symptoms involve flashbacks in which the patient relives the experience, avoidance of stimuli associated with the event, or numbing of general responsiveness.[14]

Several studies have found that many victims of violent crimes suffer from PTSD.[15] Dean Kilpatrick and his associates found that over 57 percent of all rape victims and 27 percent of nonsexual assault victims suffered from PTSD within one month after the assault.[16] Victims of crimes have reported experiencing anger, fear, anxiety, intrusive imagery and nightmares, sleep disturbance, guilt, and impairment in social functioning following the crime.[17]

It must be stressed that victims suffering from PTSD are not necessarily psychotic or deranged; rather, they are attempting to cope with a highly stressful event or series of events in their lives. An understanding and awareness of a crime's psychological impact will help peace officers obtain information and investigate the case. Investigators should understand that, like other forms of trauma, a victim suffering from PTSD may not exhibit a total disappearance of the symptoms over time; rather, the victim will feel a reduction in their frequency and intensity.[18] As these symptoms lessen, crime victims may be able to resume their places in society but they will often harbor terrifying memories. Law enforcement officers can assist victims in this transition by being sensitive to their needs, concerns, and fears.

INTERROGATIONS

The key to success in interrogating suspects is careful preparation. Just as preparation for interviewing witnesses is necessary, a complete review of all facts is a requirement for an effective interrogation. As with many aspects of police work, interrogation is more of an art than a science; however, certain broad guidelines will assist officers in this area.

Unlike in the movies, successful interrogations do not always end with a confession. Statements given by a suspect may be exculpatory in nature. That is, the suspect may deny any wrongdoing or guilt. The suspect may also admit guilt, but plead justification for those actions. Finally, an interrogation may produce a complete confession. The various degrees of statements that come from an interrogation require investigating officers to effectively utilize their communication skills to the fullest extent possible.

Interrogations should occur in a location that is free from distractions or interruptions. Most modern police departments have rooms that are designated as interview/interrogation rooms. Many are equipped with tape recorders and some have one-way mirrors so superiors or other officers working on the case can view the questioning. These rooms should be sparsely furnished, well-lit, and secure.

Numerous interrogation techniques are available to police officers. Normally, an interrogation is conducted by two officers. One officer is the primary interrogator and the second officer acts as a recorder/witness. Depending on the suspect's reaction, the officers may switch roles during the interrogation. The officers should agree before the interrogation which role each of them will take. Following is a brief summary of some of the more common interrogation techniques.

Factual This is a straightforward approach in which the officer points out all the facts that show the suspect committed the crime. The officer explains the nature of the evidence and how it conclusively proves the suspect committed the act. The officer then explains that the suspect's only alternative is to cooperate with the police and that it is in the suspect's self-interest to do so. The interrogation should be conducted in a businesslike manner, with little or no emotion displayed by the officer. The officer should not make any deals or indicate that the suspect's cooperation will be brought to the attention of the district attorney.

Sympathetic In this technique, the officer acts understanding toward the suspect's position or justification for carrying out the acts. The officer should speak in a mild voice, sit close to the suspect, and may want to occasionally touch the suspect in an understanding way. This approach offers the defendant a friendly face during the interrogation.

Face-Saving or Justification The officer using this approach encourages the suspect to state the reason for committing the act. Again, the officer should never indicate that the defendant will receive a lesser sentence or go free after explaining the reasons for the act. The officer can, however, ask questions in such a manner as to imply that what the suspect did was a natural, everyday occurrence—that anyone facing the same set of facts would do the same thing.

These interrogation techniques are usually not employed in a strict, mechanical method. The officer may have to switch from one approach to another depending on the suspect's reaction or mental state. Veteran police officers understand the need to remain flexible in this critical area of law enforcement investigation and utilize their interpersonal and communication skills to the maximum.

How the suspect's statement is recorded affects the communication process between the officer and the defendant. Several of the more common techniques to record a suspect's statement follow.

Interrogating Officer Records Statement This method requires the interrogating officer to take notes while conducting the interrogation. This can be distracting to both the suspect and the officer. It may interrupt the free flow of the discussion and cause the suspect to become concerned about what the officer is writing down. One advantage to this approach is that the officer is able to testify to personally recording the suspect's statement in his or her own handwriting. However, the disadvantages of this method outweigh that simple fact, and this technique is not used when two officers are available to interrogate the suspect.

Assisting Officer Records Statement This is one of the most common methods used to record the suspect's statement. The officer who is not doing the talking writes down what the defendant says during the interrogation. The problem with this approach is that unless the suspect is ready to give a complete confession, the situation might require both officers to ask questions at different times during the interrogation. An advantage of this technique is that it allows for uninterrupted questioning by one officer while the other takes notes. The questioning officer can concentrate on the suspect and not be diverted by having to write down what is said.

Statement Is Transcribed by Court Reporter This is one of the most accurate ways to record the suspect's statement. However, it is normally used only when the officers feel the suspect is ready to make a confession. Normally, the suspect has to agree to this method. The disadvantage of this approach is that it requires a certified court reporter to take the statement from the suspect. In addition, since the suspect usually has to agree to this procedure, it is not used until a confession has been obtained.

Statement Is Tape Recorded There are two alternatives available to tape recording a suspect's statement. The traditional method uses a common cassette tape recorder. With the advent and increased use of videotape recorders, more and more modern police departments are turning to this approach to record interrogations. This method may be either clandestine or obvious. The clandestine method usually places the video camera behind a one-way mirror. The obvious technique involves obtaining the suspect's permission prior to taping the interview. With either approach, the officer should state the time, date, and location of the recording.

The advantages are obvious: a video is a pictorial record of the suspect's demeanor as well as the statement. Also, videotapes are now used by average citizens, and jurors are more understanding and appreciative of the medium.

Accurately recording the suspect's statement is vital to the successful prosecution of the criminal case. The interrogating officers should ensure that the suspect is treated in a courteous manner and that the suspect's rights are preserved. Interrogating a suspect is one of the most critical stages of any criminal investigation and requires the officer to react in an appropriate manner at all times.

Interrogation skills, like interviewing skills, take time and practice to develop. However, once sharpened, they will serve the officer and the department well.

SUMMARY

Conducting an interview is an essential step in any criminal investigation. This encounter provides law enforcement with vital facts surrounding the commission of a crime. Many times, the interview will take place in an atmosphere charged with emotion. Victims of violent crimes may be under a great deal of stress and law enforcement officers must be sensitive to their plight, yet at the same time must proceed, gathering enough information to go forward with the investigation. This dilemma requires police officers to use all the communication skills they possess to obtain the necessary information.

Interrogating a suspect is more an art than a science. It is true that officers can learn the mechanics of an interrogation; however, knowing when to switch approaches comes only with experience and knowledge. No one technique will work on all suspects. The officer must understand this and pattern the interrogation accordingly. Even when interrogations do not produce confessions, they provide law enforcement with sufficient information to request the filing of charges by the prosecutor's office.

REVIEW QUESTIONS

1. Explain the rationale behind the *Miranda* decision.
2. Do you believe the *Miranda* warning is still a valid concept? Why?
3. What are some of the keys to success in interrogating a suspect?
4. How are interviews and interrogations distinguished from each other?
5. Explain some of the popular techniques used in interviewing potential witnesses.

BETTER WRITING DRILLS

The Better Writing Drills for this chapter are reviews of the previous drills and are designed to provide a capstone learning experience.

Clear Writing

Clear writing requires:

Use of the active voice
Use of common words
Use of parallelism
Correct modification
Proper pronoun reference
Conciseness

Characteristics of a Well-Written Report

A well-written report is factual, accurate, objective, complete, concise, clear, and on time. These are four basic steps to writing a good report:

1. Investigate, interview, and observe—gather the facts.
2. Record the facts by the use of field notes, and so forth.
3. Organize the information and report it in a systematic procedure.
4. Edit and proofread the report.

Evaluating a Report

In evaluating a report use the following criteria:

Is the report factual?
Is the report accurate?
Is the report objective?
Is the report both complete and concise?

Sentence Structure Checklist

Write in complete sentences; include both a subject and a verb.
Avoid sentence fragments.
Avoid complex sentences.
Do not run sentences together.
Combine only related ideas into single sentences.

Spelling Checklist

Memorize words frequently used in law enforcement reports.

Memorize frequently misspelled words.

Know the following basic spelling rules:

- *i* before *e* except after *c* or when sounded *a.*
- To make the plural of words ending in *y:* if the *y* is preceded by a vowel, add *s,* if the *y* is preceded by a consonant, change the *y* to *i* and add *es.*
- To add a suffix to words ending in silent *e:* if the suffix begins with a vowel, drop the *e;* if the suffix begins with a consonant, keep the *e.*
- If a word is one syllable or accented on the last syllable and it ends in a single vowel and a single consonant, double the final consonant before a suffix beginning with a vowel.

Capitalization Checklist

Use capital letters for:

- The first word in a sentence
- The names of specific people, members of national, political, racial, regional, or religious groups
- Geographical names
- Organizations and institutions
- Specific streets, buildings, ships, planes, trains, trademark names
- Historical periods, events, special events
- Days of the week, months, and holidays
- Titles used before a name

Do not capitalize:

- General words
- Directions
- Names of seasons
- Titles following a name
- Words showing family relationship preceded by a possessive pronoun

PRACTICAL APPLICATIONS

1. List a series of questions that are open ended. Ask a classmate to answer them. Did you obtain the information you sought when you drafted the questions?

2. Practice the various interrogation techniques and list the ones you are most comfortable using. Explain why you prefer those techniques over the other ones.

3. In each of the rows below, circle the correctly spelled word:

cornor	coroner	corenor	cornor
counselor	counseler	counsolor	conseler
continous	continuous	continnous	conitinous
disipation	disipetation	dissipaten	dissipation
environement	enveronment	environment	enviroment
exccepted	excception	excetion	exception
hurried	huryed	hurred	hurrid
horzontal	horizontal	horizontale	horizonal
hispanice	Hispanic	Hispanc	Hespanic
humeliate	humelate	humileate	humiliate

4. Rewrite the following sentences as needed:

   a. The building was burned to the ground by four juvenile kids.

   _____

   b. I detected the odor of smoldering smoke and then placed a call to the local fire department and requested that they send help.

   _____

   c. Jerry said that he had discovered his television set missing after being gone from his home only ten minutes that day.

   _____

   d. This officer attempted to contact the suspect by telephone and then in person.

   _____

   e. The suspect was taller and lived with his mother and father who were retired.

   _____

5. Define and explain the following words or terms:

   a. interview

   _____

   b. interrogation

   _____

   c. post-traumatic stress disorder

   _____

d. *Miranda* decision

_____

e. *Berkemer v. McCarty* rule

_____

WORDS TO KNOW

across	proprietor
always	secretary
assault	spoken
citizen	suffocation
column	technique
decision	transactional
dispatcher	transitory
height	urgent
laboratory	usually
male	weighty

ENDNOTES

1. 297 U.S. 278 (1936).
2. 322 U.S. 143 (1944).
3. 360 U.S. 315 (1959).
4. 378 U.S. 748 (1964).
5. 384 U.S. 436 (1966).
6. 468 U.S. 420 (1984).
7. 401 U.S. 222 (1971).
8. 470 U.S. 298 (1985).
9. 495 U.S. 292 (1990).
10. 111 S.Ct. 1246 (1991).
11. 114 S.Ct. 2350 (1994).
12. Kimberly A. Crawford, "Invoking the Miranda Right to Counsel," *FBI Law Enforcement Bulletin* 27 (Mar. 1995).
13. Anne C. Birge, "Cognitive Interview Technique: An Effective Investigative Tool," *Law and Order* (Nov. 1994): 39.
14. *Diagnostic Statistical Manual of Mental Disorders,* 4th ed. rev. [DSM-IV] (Washington, D.C.: American Psychiatric Association, 1994), 424.
15. A. W. Burgess and L. L. Holmstrom, "The Rape Trauma Syndrome," *American Journal of Psychiatry* 131 (1974): 981.

16. D. G. Kilpatrick, B. Saunders, A. Amick-McMullan, C. Best, L. Vernonen, and H. Resnick, "Victim and Crime Factors Associated with the Development of Post Traumatic Stress Disorder," *Behavioral Therapy* 20 (1989): 199.

17. D. S. Riggs, C. V. Dancu, B. S. Gershuny, D. Greenberg, and E. B. Foa, "Anger and Post-Traumatic Stress Disorder in Female Crime Victims," *Journal of Traumatic Stress* 5 (1992): 613.

18. Aphrodite Matsakis, *I Can't Get Over It, A Handbook for Trauma Survivors* (Oakland, Calif.: New Harbinger Publications, 1992).

12

Using Reports in Court

LEARNING OBJECTIVES

After reading this chapter, you should understand the following concepts:
- What you should do when preparing to testify in court.
- What is expected of witnesses during direct examination.
- What occurs during cross-examination.

KEY TERMS

Cross-examination—Is the asking of either direct or leading questions.

Direct examination—Is open ended and does not suggest the answer to the person being questioned.

Leading question—Is phrased in such a way as to suggest an answer to the person being questioned.

Numerous television shows attempt to portray what it is like in courtrooms. Police officers are sometimes shown as cool professionals who do not recant their positions under fierce cross-examination. Unfortunately, real life bears little resemblance to television. Many times, officers do become frustrated and flustered on the witness stand, especially if they have not properly prepared for the hearing. In court, officers have identified the wrong person as the perpetrator, forgotten to mention important details, and made other embarrassing and avoidable mistakes. Many of the mistakes made during court hearings are the direct result of an officer either failing to prepare for court or failing to discuss the case with the prosecutor before taking the stand.

The following dialogue is an example of what can happen in court if several key words are incorrectly spelled in the police report:

> *"Now officer, will you explain to the court why you attacked the victim after she had already been injured?"*
>
> "I did not attack the victim."
>
> *"But isn't this your signature on the report as the reporting officer?"*
>
> "Yes."
>
> *"Now, officer, your report reads 'I raped her in a blanket and called for an ambulance.'"*

"But sir, I meant *wrapped.*"

"Then your report is in error?"

"Yes sir."

"How many other errors are in your report?"[1]

INTRODUCTION

The criminal legal process begins with the apprehension of the suspect. Once an arrest is made, the officer must fill out a report, have it approved by the sergeant, and file it with the records division. The report and any follow-up will then be forwarded to the city attorney or district attorney's office for review, to determine if a criminal case should be filed.

The prosecuting attorney may reject the case for a violation of some technical rule or simply for insufficient evidence. The case may be returned to the arresting officer or to the detectives assigned to the case for additional follow-up prior to filing. Finally, the prosecutor may file the case.

Once the case is filed, there will be a series of hearings regarding the defendant's plea, bail, and willingness to settle the case. During this process, the arresting officer and assigned detectives continue to work on other cases or assignments. The legal system is notorious for moving slowly. Days, weeks, and months may pass before the officer is called to appear in court. For a police officer, the court appearance is the final step in the criminal justice process. It will tax the officer's communication skills to the limit.[2]

THE COURT APPEARANCE

Police officers—good police officers—do not simply arrive in court the day of the trial, do battle with the defense attorney, and convince the jury they are telling the truth and the defendant is lying. They prepare for court. During their careers officers can expect to testify in court about everything from simple traffic tickets to homicides. While the magnitude of the cases may be different, the principles regarding trial preparation are the same.

Preparing for Court

Prior to going to court, the officer should review, in detail, the report. The officer cannot expect to sit in front of a judge in a court trial, or a jury in a jury trial, and read the report. Citizens do not understand that the officer may have made numerous other arrests since this one. After all, the defendant's liberty is at stake and the defendant will testify to remembering the incident clearly; therefore, the reasoning goes, so should the officer. Depending on the seriousness of the case and how well the officer remembers the scene, it may be prudent to drive by it prior to coming to court. The officer should be able to pronounce the defendant's name and be familiar with any other unique pronunciations of words in the case. As will be seen, this adds to the officer's credibility.

Dress regulations vary, depending on the jurisdiction. Some departments require the officer to appear in court in uniform. Others give this discretion to the officer. Prosecutors have their own personal beliefs about how an officer should dress for court. Some prosecutors believe that the police uniform adds an aura of credibility; others believe it makes the officer look like the gestapo. If the officer is to appear in uniform, it should be clean and pressed. When wearing civilian attire, the officer should strive for a professional, conservative look. Remember, the jurors should pay attention to the testimony and not what the officer is wearing. Flashy clothes, rings, gold chains, or other out-of-the-ordinary dress may cause a juror to concentrate on the officer's clothing at a critical part of the testimony instead of listening. The officer does not have to wear a three-piece suit with white shirt, but should dress in a manner acceptable for court. Cowboy boots, jeans, or a leather miniskirt are definitely out—unless the officer was working undercover and the prosecutor believes the jury needs to see how the officer was dressed when the arrest was made.

Coordinating with the Prosecuting Attorney

The officer should attempt to contact the prosecutor on receiving the summons to appear in court. In most large cities and counties, prosecutors—like the police—are overworked and understaffed and may not return any phone calls before meeting the officer in the court hallway. The officer should not depend on the prosecutor to make the job of testifying easy. The prosecutor may not have examined the file prior to appearing in court and may be depending on the officer to carry the day. If there is a critical aspect of the case that is not evident from reading the report, the officer should ensure that the prosecutor is informed of it *prior* to the start of the trial—not just before the officer takes the stand. The reason for this is obvious: the prosecutor may be engaged in last minute plea-bargaining or may make an opening statement to the judge or jury that will later turn out to be false if not made aware of all the important facts surrounding the case.

Depending on the jurisdiction, the officer may have the opportunity to sit next to the prosecutor during the trial and act as an *investigating officer* or *trial assistant.* Instead of thinking of this experience as wasted time away from normal assignments, the officer should rejoice! This is an opportunity to observe the entire trial from start to finish. The experience gained from acting as an investigating officer on a case will improve the officer's courtroom demeanor immeasurably.

After discussing the case with the prosecutor, the officer will await his or her turn to testify. Depending on the nature of the case, and the prosecutor's preference, the officer may testify first or last. If at the counsel table as the investigating officer, the officer should remain attentive and assist the prosecutor whenever possible. If in the seats reserved for the general public, the officer should also remain attentive and professional. While jurors are not supposed to consider anything that is not admitted into evidence, they will sometimes form unofficial opinions of persons based on their observations of them. If required to remain outside the courtroom, the officer should also remain attentive and professional. In addition, the officer should avoid joking with other officers—and especially avoid laughing with the defense attorney. Jurors who observe these antics may believe that the officer is not serious about what is occurring in the courtroom and therefore may discount the officer's testimony.

Having reviewed the report, refreshed the memory, and talked with the prosecutor, the officer is ready to take the stand and testify.

TESTIFYING IN COURT

Some of us are uncomfortable standing or sitting in front of a group and talking. That is exactly what every police officer must master. There may be occasions when the officer testifies in a deserted courtroom with only the court personnel present. This might happen in a closed hearing where the officer is testifying regarding a confidential informant. However, the great majority of the officer's testimony will occur in public. Moreover, the officer will be subjected to cross-examination by the defense attorney, who will attempt to destroy the officer's credibility.

Even if we did not belong to the debating team in high school or college, with proper training all of us can learn to communicate in a professional manner while testifying. This oral skill can be mastered with practice, if the officer is familiar with the purposes of both direct examination and cross-examination. The following sections briefly discuss this aspect of the criminal justice process.

Direct Examination

To testify in court effectively, all officers should understand the aims or goals of direct examination. There are two generally accepted objectives that most prosecutors attempt to satisfy during all direct examinations:

1. Present all legally sufficient evidence to support the charges filed against the defendant.
2. Convince the factfinder of the integrity of the evidence and, ultimately, the truth of the charge.

Direct examination is the prosecutor's opportunity to present favorable evidence to the jury. The officer is responsible for telling the truth and leaving the jury with a good impression of professionalism and honesty. Many prosecutors hand lists to lay witnesses outlining what is expected of them during direct and cross-examination. Unfortunately, prosecutors assume that since police officers have been through academy or other formal training they understand what occurs in a courtroom. This is not necessarily the case. Following is a list of what have been called the "Ten Commandments" for witnesses[3]:

1. *Tell the Truth* In a trial, as in all other matters, honesty comes first.
2. *Don't Guess* If you don't know, say so.
3. *Be Sure You Understand the Question* You cannot possibly give a truthful and accurate answer unless you understand the question.
4. *Take Your Time and Answer the Question Asked* Give the question such thought as is required to understand it, formulate your answer, and then give the answer.
5. *Give a Loud, Audible Answer* Everything you say is being recorded. Don't nod your head *yes* or *no.*
6. *Don't Look for Assistance When You Are on the Stand* If you think you need help, request it from the judge.
7. *Beware of Questions Involving Distance and Time* If you make an estimate, make sure everyone understands that you are making an estimate.
8. *Be Courteous* Answer *Yes* or *No,* and address the judge as *Your Honor.*
9. *If Asked If You Have Talked to the Prosecutor, Admit It Freely If You Have Done So.*
10. *Avoid Joking and Wisecracks* A lawsuit is a serious matter.

These commandments are as valid for a seasoned police officer as they are for a rookie. Each rule is based on both common sense and years of court experience by prosecutors.

The first and most basic rule of testimony requires that the officer tell the truth. While it appears obvious that peace officers should always tell the truth, reality and emotions can sometimes cause officers to slant their testimony in order to assist the prosecutor or to ensure that the defendant is portrayed in a bad light. Failure to testify truthfully has several consequences. The most obvious issue is that the officer is sworn to tell the truth. Violation of this oath can lead to criminal charges or the destruction of the officer's reputation. Additionally, the officer's credibility may be destroyed in front of the court or jury, with the result that they disbelieve all of the officer's testimony and acquit the defendant. This is the exact opposite of what the officer intended when slanting or stretching the truth to help out the prosecutor or place the defendant in an unfavorable light. Who can forget the problems caused in the O. J. Simpson case when it was learned that Detective Furman of the LAPD had "forgotten" using racial slurs in the past.

Very close to the first rule is the second, which requires that the officer not try to help the case by guessing. If the officer is unsure, a simple statement to that effect is sufficient. Additionally, this type of statement shows the jury that the officer is human and may not have all the answers to every single question.

The third rule simply requires that the officer understand the exact question that is asked. This appears simple at first glance; however, many times attorneys will ask several questions in one sentence. If the officer is unsure of the exact question, a request should be made to repeat or clarify the question.

The fourth rule requires the officer to think through both the question and answer before blurting out a response. There is nothing wrong with taking a few seconds to form your answer in your mind before responding to the question.

The fifth requirement mandates that the officer answer in a loud and clear voice. Remember, appellate courts have only the written transcript of what occurred when they review a case on appeal. The court reporter will not transcribe a nod of the head or estimate the distance between the officer's hands when demonstrating a gesture or action of either the officer or the defendant. If the officer is going to use motions during the testimony, they should be accompanied by an accurate verbal description.

The sixth commandment may seem harsh, but it is there for the officer's benefit. The officer must understand that no one but the judge can intervene during direct- or cross-examination. The attorneys may raise objections, but the court must decide if they are valid or not.

The seventh rule is one that every rookie will violate at least once. Typically, the officer may state a distance during direct examination. For example, in response to a question by the prosecutor regarding the distance between the officer and the defendant, the officer may state, "The defendant was twenty feet from me when I observed the weapon." On cross-examination, the defense attorney may ask the officer to point out an object in court that is 20 feet from the witness stand. If the officer is mistaken about that distance, the defense attorney will go to great pains to point it out and will end up asking how the officer could be certain about the distance between the officer and the defendant on the night in question when he or she cannot even make an accurate estimate in the calm and secure setting of a courtroom.

The eighth commandment is basically common sense, but can also build an officer's credibility. The officer should be seen as a professional and not someone who does not respect authority.

The ninth rule ties in with the first rule in that it requires the officer to answer every question truthfully. There is absolutely nothing improper in discussing the case with the prosecutor before testifying.

The last commandment goes to the officer's credibility. The defendant's liberty is at stake during the trial. The officer should be professional and calm in answering every question.

Once called to testify, the officer should approach the witness chair or, as it is sometimes called, witness box, and turn to the clerk or judge to be sworn in. The officer will be asked to swear or affirm to tell the truth, the whole truth, and nothing but the truth. Once sworn in, the prosecutor, clerk, or judge will tell the officer to be seated. The officer should wait for this invitation, as it shows respect for the court and allows the prosecutor to appear to be in control of the courtroom.

Once the officer is seated, the prosecutor will ask a series of questions regarding the officer's knowledge of the crime or the defendant. This is known as *direct examination.* Following is a series of preliminary questions most prosecutors will use to start the questioning:

- Would you state your full name for the record?
- What is your occupation?
- How long have you been employed by the X police department?
- On the (date and time in question) what was your assignment?
- On that date and time did you observe anything unusual?
- At what location did you observe this occurrence?
- Is that location in the (city, county, state) of X?

The purpose of these questions is to allow the officer to become comfortable on the stand and give the jury some background information regarding the officer. It also sets the stage for the more critical testimony regarding the officer's observations and reactions. In some jurisdictions these questions are known as *foundational questions,* in that they establish the officer's jurisdiction and authority to act.

When a party—in this instance, the people of the state through the prosecutor—calls a witness, they are allowed to ask only direct questions (with some minor exceptions that are not relevant to this text). This is accomplished through direct examination. A direct question is open ended and does not suggest the answer to the person being questioned. Once the prosecutor has finished with direct examination, the defense attorney has a right to cross-examine. Cross-examination allows asking either direct or leading questions. A *leading question* is phrased in such a way as to suggest an answer to the person being questioned.

After establishing the jurisdiction for the officer to act, the prosecutor will question the witness about his or her knowledge of the crime. The officer should listen to each question and ensure that he or she understands what is being asked. If it is not clear what the question is, the officer should state that and ask the prosecutor to restate the question. "I'm not certain I understand your question; would you please restate it?" is one way to ask for clarification. A review of the previous chapters will indicate that such a question is a form of feedback.

If the question is understood, the officer should pause for a second and then answer. This pause should follow every question; as will be discussed, it becomes very important during cross-examination.

In answering the question, the officer should only answer exactly what was asked. Following is an example of an officer answering more than was asked:

> *Did you observe anyone at that location?*
>
> Yes, as I pulled up to the service station, he saw me and fled from the scene. I then lost sight of him for several minutes, but observed him one block from the scene of the crime.

Not only is the officer's response defective on several grounds, it creates more questions than it answers. Furthermore, without clarifying some of the issues in the officer's answer, the prosecutor may have opened the door for the defense attorney to question whether the defendant was really the same person who fled from the service station. Following is a specific series of questions dealing with the issues the officer raised:

> *Did you observe anyone at that location?*
> Yes, I did.
>
> *Who did you observe?*
> I saw the defendant.
>
> *Would you point to that person if he is in court and, for the record, describe what he is wearing?*
> Yes, it is the person sitting next to the defense attorney, wearing a blue suit.
>
> *How far away were you when you saw the defendant?*
> I was about fifteen feet from him.
>
> *What was he doing when you first saw him?*
> He was backing out of the service station office.
>
> *What, if anything, did he do next?*
> He looked towards my marked patrol vehicle and fled.
>
> *Where did he go?*
> He ran south on Broadway Street.
>
> *What did you do at that time?*
> I entered the service station to check on the welfare of the people inside and was informed by Mr. Smith that the defendant had just robbed them at gunpoint.[4]

Once you heard this, what did you do?
I called for backup on my police radio.

Is that the only thing you did—call for backup?
No, I broadcast a description of the defendant, including his height, weight, color, and clothing.

Where did you receive that information?
I observed the defendant when I drove into the location, and broadcast that information.

What did you do next?
I proceeded south on Broadway and observed the defendant standing behind some boxes in the alley.

After you saw him, what did you do?
I pulled my service weapon and ordered him to put his hands in the air and turn around.

The difference between the two sets of questions is apparent. The second set provides the jury with more complete facts surrounding the incident and establishes why the officer could recognize the defendant even though she lost sight of him for several minutes.

Cross-Examination

Once the officer has finished answering the questions posed by the prosecutor, the defense attorney has the right to ask questions on cross-examination. Unlike trials in the movies, cross-examination very seldom breaks down witnesses and gets them to recant their previous testimony. Rather, it is a series of questions designed to attack the credibility of witnesses by showing weaknesses in their original testimony or by establishing a motive or bias on their part.

There are several purposes to cross-examination. All officers should be aware of these objectives, to better understand the questions being asked them by defense attorneys. Depending on the jurisdiction, some questions or issues may not be raised on cross-examination.[5] However, the general objectives of cross-examination include, but are not limited to, the following points:

1. To develop favorable matters that were left unsaid on direct examination.
2. To introduce all of a conversation or document, if the witness has testified to only a part of the content.
3. To demonstrate that the witness is lying.
4. To establish that the witness could not have seen or heard what he or she has claimed.

5. To test the witness's ability to hear, see, remember, and relate facts with accuracy.
6. To establish the witness's bias or prejudice.
7. To establish any interest the witness may have in the outcome of the case.
8. To impair the credibility of the witness.
9. To impeach the witness by any means permitted by law.

Just as with direct examination, the officer should pause before answering any question. This pause is critical, in that it allows the prosecutor to object to the question and prevent its answer from coming before the jury. There are numerous tactics or techniques that defense attorneys can and will use to discredit the officer's testimony. However, this is not a chapter on courtroom survival. Rather, it concerns communication; therefore, only general principles will be discussed in this area.

The officer should know the facts surrounding the case. It is not professional and it is embarrassing for the officer to say, "I don't recall, but I put it in my report." Rest assured, the defense attorney will know the facts—and will have the opportunity to read the report again while the officer is testifying. In addition, the defense attorney has the defendant's version to draw on. While defendants do not always tell their attorneys the complete truth, the defense attorney is provided with another perspective on the facts which can be used to attack the officer.

Always maintain a professional, courteous attitude. Some attorneys will argue with witnesses, others will be condescending, and some may even sneer. No matter what tactic is utilized, the officer should never, ever lose his or her temper. The officer must be prepared for these types of defense ploys and respond in a positive manner. This reinforces in the jury's mind that the officer is a professional simply doing a job.

If the officer makes a mistake during testimony and is caught by the defense attorney, the officer should readily admit to the mistake. There is nothing that damages credibility more than letting a defense attorney lead an officer down a path of rationalizations in an attempt to justify an obvious mistake.

The officer's voice and body language should convey the attitude of a calm professional. The voice should be loud enough for all the jurors to hear, but not so loud as to distract from what is being said. The officer should avoid squirming on the witness stand. If the testimony has proceeded for over two hours and the officer has to use the rest room, the officer should politely ask for a brief recess.

The officer should not despair if it appears that the defense attorney is "winning." After cross-examination, the prosecutor is allowed to conduct *redirect*. This is the prosecutor's opportunity to clarify any issues that may have been raised on cross-examination.

Preparing for and testifying in court are everyday experiences for some officers. Even when it becomes a common occurrence, the officer must understand that unless the information can be conveyed to the jury in the proper manner, all the work done during the arrest, questioning, and charging of the defendant may be wasted. This experience can be one of the most challenging and exciting aspects of police work.

SUMMARY

The law enforcement officer's testimony in court is the final step in the criminal justice procedure. The officer should carefully prepare for this event and always remember to present a professional image to the court and jury. The officer's professional reputation—and the department's—goes on the line every time the officer testifies.

Preparing to testify is as important as the actual testimony. The officer must never assume the case will be easy or that the defendant's attorney will not attack the officer's credibility. Whenever possible, the officer should discuss the case with the prosecuting attorney before entering the courtroom.

Direct examination and cross-examination have distinct purposes. The officer should be prepared for both types of questioning and follow the "Ten Commandments" as closely as possible. There are various techniques that all officers should remember when testifying. These will become second nature to most officers after they have testified in court several times.

REVIEW QUESTIONS

1. What is the most appropriate attire for an officer testifying in court? Why?
2. Which of the "Ten Commandments" is the most important? Why?
3. If you had to delete one of the "Ten Commandments," which one would you delete? Why?
4. Which is more important—direct examination or cross-examination? Why?
5. What effect can a simple reporting error have on an officer's testimony?

BETTER WRITING DRILLS

Editing is a critical part of any written communications. Editing requires more than just using the spellchecker on your word processing program. Editing is rewriting to improve the document. Ernest Hemingway once stated that he rewrote the last paragraph of *For Whom the Bells Toll* 39 times. When asked what problems he was having with the last paragraph, he merely stated that the problem was with the "words."

Terri LeClercq developed certain tips that writers can use to shorten a document and to "power edit" their work.[6] Her suggestions are as follows:

- If possible, eliminate qualifying adverbs such as "very" and "many" that mask weak verbs and adjectives.
- Since "there" is generally followed by a "to be" verb, the weak and wordy combination can be replaced by the use of a stronger verb.
- Often, "to be" verbs (*is, are, was, were, am, will be, has, had, have, be,* and *been*) can be replaced with vibrant verbs that carry a stronger message.
- Common words that often can be eliminated include *that, the, by, of,* and *to. Draft:* Writers can gain power by editing unnecessary verbiage. *Better:* Writers can gain power editing unnecessary verbiage.
- Some words and phrases are inherently redundant, e.g., *co-conspirator, in order to, the fact that, the question as to whether, because, unless and until,* and *lease agreement.*

PRACTICAL APPLICATIONS

1. Form five-person teams and require everyone to write down their observations for a 30-minute period when they are alone. Have each member of the team testify in front of the others regarding their observations. How accurate is the testimony?
2. Watch a television show in which an officer testifies. How many of the "Ten Commandments" did the officer violate? Be prepared to explain what occurred, and why you believe the testimony was flawed.
3. In each of the rows below, circle the correctly spelled word:

anxeity	anxiety	anixety	anexity
bagage	baggage	bagaged	baggageed
benefitted	benefited	benfited	benfeted
carpose	coprse	coper	corpse
coroborate	corroberate	corroborate	corroborete
begueath	bequaeth	bequeth	bequeath
behavior	baveor	bahevior	bahavor
corresponde	correspond	correponde	corespond
councelman	cuncilman	councileman	councilman
corperal	coparel	corporal	corparele

4. Rewrite the following sentences as needed:

   a. The very young child victim wore a bright red colorful shoes and a bright red colorful dress.

b. Today is worse than yesterday which was worse than tomorrow and both were better than friday.

_____

c. The crooked illegal card dealer deal the card from the bottom of the deck.

_____

d. Please bringed the coffee to me when you are going by home.

_____

e. The report written by this officer contain several mistakes and it won't happen again.

_____

5. Define and explain the following words or terms:
   a. direct examination

_____

   b. cross-examination

_____

   c. leading question

_____

   d. foundational questions

_____

   e. redirect examination

_____

WORDS TO KNOW

agency	computer
alcohol	discrepancy
among	receipt
analyze	recognize
anger	records
answered	restaurant
attendance	specimen
audible	subject
chronological	suspect
clothing	tolerate

ENDNOTES

1. Adapted from Tom E. Kakonis and Donald K. Hanzek, *A Practical Guide to Police Report Writing* (New York: McGraw-Hill, 1977).

2. Much of the material in this chapter is based on the authors' experiences as a prosecutor, defense attorney, and police officer.

3. Adapted from "Direct Examination: A Prosecutor's Workshop," County of San Diego, Calif., District Attorney's Office (November 15, 1975).

4. Some jurisdictions might consider Mr. Smith's statement to the officer to be hearsay. However, others will admit it, not for the truth of the matter stated, but for the limited purpose of showing the officer's state of mind.

5. "Cross Examination: Trial Techniques Training Program," County of San Diego, Calif., District Attorney's Office (January 29, 1977).

6. Terri LeClercq, "Power Editing," *Texas Bar Journal,* March, 1994, pp. 22–24.

Index